THE
SOCIAL INTERPRETATION OF
THE FRENCH REVOLUTION

THE WILES LECTURES
GIVEN AT THE QUEEN'S UNIVERSITY
BELFAST, 1962

THE SOCIAL
INTERPRETATION
OF THE FRENCH
REVOLUTION

BY

ALFRED COBBAN

CAMBRIDGE
AT THE UNIVERSITY PRESS
1968

PUBLISHED BY
THE SYNDICS OF THE CAMBRIDGE UNIVERSITY PRESS

Bentley House, 200 Euston Road, London, N.W.1
American Branch: 32 East 57th Street, New York, N.Y. 10022

© CAMBRIDGE UNIVERSITY PRESS 1964

Standard Book Numbers:
521 04679 3 clothbound
521 09548 4 paperback

First published 1964
Reprinted   1965
First paperback
        edition 1968

First printed in Great Britain by Latimer Trend & Co. Ltd, Whitstable
Reprinted in Great Britain by Hazell Watson & Viney Ltd, Aylesbury,
Bucks

CONTENTS

PREFACE

I<small>T</small> is only fitting that this book should begin with an expression of the author's gratitude to the founder of the Wiles Lectures, to the Vice-Chancellor of The Queen's University, Belfast, and to Professor Michael Roberts and his colleagues, both for the invitation to deliver the lectures and for everything that makes them such an enjoyable occasion for the lecturer. I must also thank my friends and fellow-students of the history of the French Revolution, who honoured me by attending the lectures and discussing them with me afterwards.

The intention of the founder of the Wiles Lectures, as I understand it, was not to endow detailed research, but to promote reflection about historical problems. In my lectures, and in the book which is based on them, I have tried to meet this requirement while recognising the risks it brings with it. In the first place, this is bound to be in some respects a critical activity. Historical research can be, and perhaps usually is, done within the limits of an accepted pattern. Reflection about history brings with it the possibility of wanting to change the pattern. When, as in the case of the French Revolution, it is a well-established pattern, consolidated by a series of great historians, with long accepted theoretical implications, any attempt to question it is likely to meet with automatic and authoritative resistance. The resistance will be all the stronger if it seems that a formula which appeared to explain the revolution satisfactorily is being discarded, without another being provided to take its place. This, I fear, is what I am doing. Indeed, it would be self-defeating if I were merely to try to replace one dogma with another.

The positive views I have expressed are tentative throughout. They represent what the evidence—or rather such part of it as I have been able to examine— seems to indicate. I am acutely aware that I am far from having exhausted even the printed sources available. There are also a host of local studies, in the admirable local historical journals of France, which can throw important light on general problems, but which historians, perhaps under the illusion that any unprinted document, however insignificant, is a more valuable historical source than anything printed, however important, have been apt to neglect. I have not attempted to make an exhaustive study of any single aspect of the revolution. I am quite prepared to discover that on more than one point the samples I have been able to take are not representative and have misled me. My object has been to examine the broad bases of revolutionary history and on these to adduce only sufficient evidence to suggest the need for a new approach. I have confined myself to social problems because these are the ones which, it seems to me, have most relevance to the present state of historiography.

Finally, one cannot criticise an historical interpretation without appearing to criticise the historians who have held it. If I have been led to disagree sometimes with the interpretation of a great historian like Georges Lefebvre, or with that of historians, such—to name only two—as

M. Bouloiseau and M. Soboul, for whose work I have great respect, this in no way represents a failure to recognize its value. In particular, it should be obvious to any reader that without the work of Lefebvre this book would be greatly impoverished. If I have disagreed with some of his interpretations, it has often been on the ground of evidence supplied by himself. This, I fear, might not have given him pleasure, but it is testimony to him none the less.

UNIVERSITY COLLEGE   A.C.
LONDON
January 1963

KEY TO REFERENCES

The full title of books and articles is given the first time each one appears in the notes. For the first references to titles subsequently abridged see as follows—

L'ancien moniteur [49].
Aulard, *La Révolution française et le régime féodal* [42].
Bigo, *Les bases historiques de la finance moderne* [85].
Bligny-Bondurand, *Cahiers de Nîmes* [100].
Bois, *Paysans de l'Ouest* [19].
Boissonade, *Cahiers d'Angoulême* [99].
Bouloiseau, *Cahiers de Rouen* [37].
Bourgin, *Le Partage des biens communaux* [110].
Braesch, *1789, l'année cruciale* [63].
Carré, *La Noblesse de France et l'opinion publique* [29].
Champion, *La France d'après les cahiers* [37].
Chassin, *Les Élections et les cahiers de Paris* [31].
Cobb, *Les armées révolutionnaires* [124].
Crouzet, 'Les conséquences économiques de la Révolution' [73].
Desplaces de Charmasse, *Cahiers d'Autun* [34].
Doniol, *La Révolution française et la féodalité* [36].
Étienne, *Cahiers de Metz et de Nancy* [51].
Ferrières, Marquis de, *Correspondance inédite* [33].
Ford, *Robe and Sword* [46].
Forster, *Nobility of Toulouse* [30].
Fourastié, *Cahiers de Cahors* [46].
Garaud, *La Révolution et la propriété foncière* [28].
Gerbaux et Schmidt, *Comités d'agriculture et de commerce* [63].
Grille, *Introduction aux Mémoires* [29].
Guérin, *Bourgeois et 'bras nus'* [11].
Herbert, *Fall of Feudalism* [46].
Jouanne, *Cahiers d'Alençon* [50].
Labasse, *La commerce des soies à Lyon* [75].
Labrousse, *La Crise de l'économie française* [44].

Laurent, *Reims et la région rémoise* [37].

Lefebvre, *Études* [8].

Lefebvre, 'Le mythe de la Révolution française' [10].

Lefebvre, *Paysans du Nord* [38].

Lhéritier, *La fin de l'ancien régime* [60].

Lizerand, *Le régime rural de l'ancienne France* [27].

Loriquet, *Cahiers du Pas-de-Calais* [34].

Martin, *Cahiers de Mirecourt* [38].

Mège, *Cahiers d'Auvergne* [49].

Méthivier, *L'ancien régime* [36].

Nussbaum, *Commercial policy in the French Revolution* [69].

Picard, *Les Cahiers de 1789* [62].

Plaisse, *La baronnie de Neubourg* [33].

Reinhard, 'Sur l'histoire de la Révolution française' [25].

Rudé, *The Crowd in the French Revolution* [122].

Sagnac et Caron, *Les comités des droits féodaux* [27].

Saint-Jacob, *Les paysans de la Bourgogne* [45].

Savina et Bernard, *Cahiers de Quimper et de Concarneau* [46].

Sée, *L'Évolution commerciale et industrielle* [63].

Sentou, 'Impôts et citoyens actifs' [30].

Soboul, *Précis* [8].

Soboul, *Les sans-culottes parisiens* [122].

CHAPTER I

THE PRESENT STATE OF HISTORY

THE historian who is called upon to deliver the Wiles Lectures is invited not so much to write the history of his chosen period or subject as to reflect upon it. There are possibly still some who will regard such reflection as an historical perversion, if not the original historical sin, and regret the days of supposed innocence when the historian could gaze on all his works and find them good, before the serpent of ideological doubt had entered his paradise and tempted him to speculate on his own presuppositions and those of other historians. Some perhaps still look back nostalgically—though they might not put it in this way—to that fairy-tale world when all the historian had to do was to release the facts from their enchanted sleep in archive or record, blow off the dust, and waving his pen, like the wand of a fairy in a Maeterlinck play, bid them speak for themselves. 'It is not I who write,' declared Fustel de Coulanges in a well-known phrase, 'but history which writes through me.' So doubtless the professor in *Lucky Jim* believed when he lifted his telephone and intoned 'History speaking'.

That happy time, if it ever existed, is over. It is now a platitude that history is made—of course not arbitrarily—by historians, and changes when they change and as their world changes. The process has often been a slow one and not easily perceptible, but there have also been periods of rapid change in the writing of history. I believe that the present may be such a period. When Taine came to London, one of the things he did was to stand, in the morning, before the gates of a great London railway terminus, when it was releasing the flood of what were not yet called commuters from the suburbs, in order, he said, to gain an impression of the collective businessman's face. The editor of an historical journal, exposed to the mass impact of the torrent of historical works that pours in on him, may have a similar illusion, and be tempted to draw from his experience conclusions as superficial as those that Taine did. For example, he might conclude that one condition for an historian's success today is to *have no footnotes*—otherwise he will never become a star of television or the Sunday papers, or a beneficiary of the book clubs. But it would be a mistake to take this as an inherent characteristic of the contemporary development of history. Rather it is a simple consequence of the pressures of commercialisation.

A more significant feature of current trends in historical writing is the appearance of an increasing number of books *about* history, and the tendency, even in historical text-books or monographs, to devote more space to historiographical discussion than would have been allowed until quite recently. This, I believe, reflects a growing awareness of the contribution of the historian himself, his personality and his ideas, to the history that he writes. It means that the Croce-Collingwood paradox that all history is contemporary history—not in any

abstruse philosophical sense, but in the plain, straight-
forward sense that it is all part of contemporary thought
—has now become a platitude. Before it comes to be so
completely accepted that it is taken for granted, and the
fact that any different view was ever possible is forgotten,
it will be worth while reminding ourselves that the view
of the historian's activity that was generally assumed in
the past generation was very different. Naturally, since it
was mostly a naïve, un-selfquestioning activity, we cannot look to historians themselves for a description of what
they were doing. An admirable account has been provided, however, by Professor Michael Oakeshott, in his
lecture 'The activity of being an historian'.[1] I have discussed this in another lecture in the same series[2] and will
therefore treat it quite briefly here. Professor Oakeshott
finds three major attributes in historical activity, and his
analysis is undoubtedly true of history as it was generally
understood during the inter-war years. First, the historian
is interested in past events for their own sake and independent of any subsequent or present events.[3] (To believe
this, all he needs is rather more than the normal capacity
for self-deception.) Secondly, he must not enquire into
origins or discuss causes, because this would be to read
history backwards.[4] (A reaction, perhaps, against taking
Edwards' notes on the causes of the Wars of the Roses
seriously.) Indeed, the idea of historical causation is a
difficult one, and has not been made easier by the recent
efforts of philosophers to explain it. One can sympathise

[1] *Historical Studies*, I, ed. T. Desmond Williams (1958), pp. 1–19.
[2] *Historical Studies*, III, ed. James Hogan (1961), pp. 1–8.
[3] *Historical Studies*, I, p. 12.
[4] *Ibid.*, p. 15.

with Professor Oakeshott's desire to discard it altogether. Moreover, he is only reflecting the natural and justifiable tendency in historical research when he tells us, 'The relation *between* events is always other events, and it is established in history by a full relation *of* the events.'[1] (Such a full relation would however require omniscience to know and eternity to narrate.) Thirdly, and this also reflects orthodox historical opinion though it is put in a paradoxical form, we must not impose present sense on past nonsense.[2] This is not to say that history is a tale told by an idiot—but all the same it is an idiotic tale. The historian's god is chance. Cleopatra's nose, the Duchess of Marlborough's gloves, the Holy Roman Emperor's mushrooms, Hitler sending a dispatch a day later than he should have sent it—these are the true stuff of history. And the task of the historian is to accumulate more and more of such facts and put them in chronological order. His not to reason why; indeed, he must not reason at all. His world is an academic Garden of Eden, a nudist's paradise of naked facts, in which he may sport, innocent not only of the ideas of good and evil (as Professor Oakeshott and others have told us, the historian must conscientiously avoid moral judgements), but innocent of any ideas at all.

Of course, it must be recognised that not all historians have been able to live up to this austere ideal. Bury found himself tempted to ask what was the use of the accumulation of statistics, the publication of trivial records, the labour expended on minute criticism. Rapidly putting

---

[1] M. Oakeshott, *Experience and its Modes* (1933), p. 143.
[2] *Cf. Historical Studies,* I, pp. 18–19.

4

temptation behind him, he replied, 'That is not so much our business as the business of future generations. We are heaping up material and arranging it, according to the best methods we know. . . . Our work is to be used by future ages.'[1] This was weak: he should frankly have admitted that it was not to be used at all. Other distinguished historians have also betrayed their feeling that something might be wrong with the kind of history which Sir Maurice Powicke described as 'a pedantic chase after the insignificant'[2] and Marc Bloch as '*le goût de l'infiniment petit*'.[3] More recently, Mr Barraclough has gone much farther. He has told us, 'We must seek for history an end outside itself, as it had, for example, when it was viewed as a manifestation of God's providence.'[4] This is a noble aspiration but hardly one that the historian can meet. What it calls for is a St Augustine or a Bossuet. The best the present century has been able to provide in this line is Professor Toynbee. His monumental *Study of History* is an interpretation of the course of human life and the destiny of man: it may be a philosophy of history, it is not history and we should not expect historians to provide us with a philosophy or a substitute religion.

This does not mean that we have to accept the picture of history as a simple collection of events 'organically related by successiveness, by sequence in time', to quote Sir George Clark in his introduction to the *New*

---

[1] J. B. Bury, *An Inaugural Lecture* (1903), pp. 31–2.

[2] F. M. Powicke, 'The Collection and Criticism of Original Texts' (1931), in *Modern Historians and the Study of History* (1955), p. 192.

[3] Marc Bloch, *Les caractères originaux de l'histoire rurale française*, ii, ed. R. Dauvergne (1956), p. xvii.

[4] G. Barraclough, *History in a Changing World* (1955), p. 29.

Cambridge Modern History.[1] Whatever historians may have said, or believed, no historian has ever written a history which is a simple relation of successive events. Professor Oakeshott is right: to ask for pure narrative is to ask for pure nonsense. Amid a multitude of recorded facts, some principle of selection, conscious or unconscious, is inevitable, and this principle must be an idea of some kind. Historians who imagined that they were free from the infection of ideas were those whose presuppositions were so deeply rooted as to be below the level of consciousness; they were taken for granted, assumed to be part of the nature of things and were therefore not susceptible to rational criticism. The greater English historians—Stubbs, Maitland, Acton, to mention only a few—illumined their history with a conscious and rational set of values. Some of these were inherited by their successors; but as they ceased to be rationally and consciously held they became stereotypes that were taken for granted, unconscious presuppositions, and the historians who inherited them thought in all innocence that they were free from the infection of ideas.

This was an illusion. All history involves the selection of facts and their arrangement in more than a temporal order. Even the editing of an original document is an act of discrimination, and thus a judgement reflecting the interests and values of the historian. If this is so, it is better that we should recognise it. To know that there are theoretical assumptions behind the history we write is not to reduce history to the expression of a theory, but to

[1] *New Cambridge Modern History*, I (1957), General Introduction, p. xxi.

take a necessary step to its emancipation from the *a priori* and towards really critical history.

Of course, not all topics or periods are equally subject to the influence of theoretical presuppositions, even if the history of none can be totally immune from it. This book has to discuss a phase in the history of Europe—the French Revolution—which, perhaps more than any other, has had its history written in ideological terms.[1] And this fact is of broad historiographical significance, for the revolution is the strategic centre of modern history. Its interpretation is crucial both for the understanding of the age of social change which preceded it and of the period—now nearly two centuries—of revolution which has followed. This is my justification for beginning with a brief discussion of the ideological problem of revolutionary history.

---

[1] *Cf.* my *Historians and the Causes of the French Revolution* (1958).

CHAPTER II

HISTORY AND SOCIOLOGY

THE established theory of the French Revolution, put forward in a broad sense at the time by the actors in the revolutionary drama, expanded into a general historical theory by the historians of the French Restoration, and taken for granted in most of the work that has since been done on the history of the revolution, is put in clear and concise language by one of the greatest of French historians of this century. 'The revolution', writes Georges Lefebvre, 'is only the crown of a long economic and social evolution which has made the bourgeoisie the mistress of the world.'[1] M. Albert Soboul, in an excellent précis of the history of the revolution, repeats Lefebvre's formula in almost the same words. He makes it more explicit, however, when he adds that though this idea was first proclaimed clearly by the bourgeois historians of the Restoration, they failed to see the essential fact. This was 'that the revolution is explained in the last analysis by a contradiction between the relations of production and the character of the productive forces'.[2] With such views we seem to be at the opposite extreme from that represented by those historians who tried, if unavailingly, to take the meaning out of history. Lefebvre

[1] G. Lefebvre, *Études sur la Révolution française* (1954), p. 246.
[2] A. Soboul, *Précis d'histoire de la Révolution française* (1962), p. 8.

and M. Soboul seem to be putting almost too much meaning back into it, when they reduce the greatest happening in modern history to the deterministic operation of an historical law.

Being an historical law, though it was first detected by historians of the French Revolution, it had to be capable of application to the interpretation of other revolutions. Thus, the Russian historian, Porchnev, among others, has seen the troubles in seventeenth-century France in terms of a feudal society under attack from the people; while the English civil war also has been widely interpreted as a bourgeois revolt against feudalism. After a period when such views had the authority of almost unchallengeable orthodoxy, they have come recently under serious criticism as an attempt to force historical evidence within the strait-jacket of a pre-conceived theory. 'Porchnev', writes Professor Mousnier, 'was determined at all costs to bring correct facts, justly observed and appreciated relationships, within the limits of a Marxist theory that the material itself exploded.'[1] In the historiography of the English civil war the explosion has already occurred, and it has blown up the supposed bourgeois revolution, leaving aristocracy and gentry, royal officials, lawyers, merchants, people, rising and falling classes, feudal and bourgeois society, landowners and peasants, scattered in fragments about monographs and text-books.

Some eight or nine years ago I suggested that the same process of disintegration was likely to take place in the history of the French Revolution, and that the inter-

[1] R. Mousnier, 'Recherches sur les soulèvements populaires en France avant la Fronde', *Revue d'histoire moderne et contemporaine*, v (1958), p. 83.

pretation of the revolution in terms of the overthrow of feudalism by the bourgeoisie, always rather meaningless, was becoming increasingly incompatible with the results of modern research.[1] This suggestion, although it was based in part on the results of Lefebvre's own researches, met with his criticism.[2] The suggestion that the theory of the revolution as the overthrow of feudalism by the bourgeoisie was a myth, he took to be equivalent to a denial of the whole actuality of the revolution. At the same time, he agreed that, in a different and Sorelian sense, it was indeed a myth. 'The convocation of the États généraux', he wrote, 'was a "bonne nouvelle": it proclaimed the birth of a new society in conformity with justice, in which life would be better.'[3] A Dutch historian has subsequently observed, not I feel unjustly, that in this defence of the traditional view of the revolution the great French historian went some way towards justifying a different criticism, that of Professor Talmon,[4] by identifying the revolution with the kind of political Messianism for which Talmon condemned it.[5]

Indeed, it is difficult to avoid the conclusion that the orthodox theory of the revolution has now assumed some

---

[1] *The Myth of the French Revolution* (1955), pp. 8 ff.

[2] G. Lefebvre, 'Le mythe de la Révolution française', *Annales historiques de la Révolution française*, no. 145 (1956), pp. 337–45.

[3] *Ibid.*, p. 345.

[4] J. L. Talmon, *The Origins of Totalitarian Democracy* (1952).

[5] B. W. Schaper, 'Robespierre opnieuw bekeken balaus van een bi-centenaire', *Tidschrift voor Geschiedenis* (1960), p. 23. H. Calvet warned that under the influence of abstract sociological theories history would become 'une sorte de mythologie où les dieux nouveaux, maîtres absolus du sort des hommes et de leurs actions, s'appelleraient esprit de classe ou mouvement des prix'. 'Sur l'histoire de la Révolution française', *Revue d'histoire moderne et contemporaine* (1954), p. 305.

of the characteristics of a religious belief. M. Guérin gave his reply to the critics of his *Bourgeois et 'bras-nus'* the title *'Bataille autour de notre mère'*, invoking with filial devotion 'the great Revolution, mother of the revolutions of the present and the future'.[1] The East German historian, W. Markov, sketching the last days of the left-wing agitator, Roux, could say, 'Jacques Roux had already found, while he was writing these lines, at Bicêtre, *le terme de sa passion*'.[2] And so on. This tendency of the Marxist theory of the revolution to culminate in a sort of semi-religious exaltation is far from being an accident. Marxism is a philosophy of history: its strength is that, like all philosophies of history, it embodies a view of the nature and ends of human existence. In other words, it is a sort of secular religion.

However, the Marxist theory of the revolution would not have had the same general appeal if it had not also been something else. If one source of the strength of Marxism is the satisfaction it can give to the human desire for a purpose to justify and provide an end for the life of the human animal, another is its appearance of providing a scientific statement of the laws of social development. As well as a philosophy of history, it offers a theory of sociology. Particularly in the latter capacity it evidently appealed to Georges Lefebvre, who seems to have come to believe, in his later years, that Marxism could provide both a theoretical basis for his researches and a conclusion he could draw from them.

[1] D. Guérin, *La Lutte des classes sous la première république: bourgeois et 'bras-nus'* (1793–97) (1946); *La Nouvelle réforme* (1958), p. 217.

[2] W. Markov, 'Les Jacquesroutins', *Annales historiques de la Révolution française*, XXXII (1960), p. 165.

The relations of history and social theory need not be discussed, however, simply in terms of Marxism, though this is the sociological theory that has so far had the greatest influence on historical studies. There is now a strong, and possibly a growing tendency, for non-Marxist historians also to look for explanations to what in a general sense may be called sociology. This tendency has recently been put in forceful language by Dr E. H. Carr. 'The more sociological history becomes, and the more historical sociology becomes', he writes, 'the better for both.'[1] The present trend towards faith in the powers of sociology is perhaps the nemesis of a period when it was believed that history could be written in the form of a simple collection of unique events related to one another only by successiveness in time. On the other hand, it may be that the absence of sociological theory is the explanation of what now seems inadequate, or superficial, in what is sometimes called naïve history. The possible contribution of sociology, even apart from Marxist sociology, to historical study needs to be considered seriously.

In the first place, however, there is the difficulty that any general theory of sociology must also be, like Marxism, a philosophy of history. Marxism, it has been said, is not a theory of classes but a theory of the evolution of classes;[2] just as Toynbee has given us a theory of the history of civilisations, not a theory of civilisation. Now the inherent assumption in any philosophy of history is that the evolution of humanity is a single process; but if

[1] E. H. Carr, *What is History?* (1961), p. 60.
[2] J. Schlumpeter, *Imperialism, Social Classes* (ed. of 1955), p. 102.

this is allowed, then there cannot be a scientific law about it, because as Professor Popper has pointed out, a scientific law cannot be deduced from a single example.[1] Even if it could be, the relation between history and any general theory of sociology is one which essentially prohibits scientific verification. {The sociological historian uses his theory as the criterion for the selection of the relevant historical facts, and then on the basis of those selected facts he illustrates and confirms the theory by which they have been selected.} Part of the fascination of general sociological theories is that success is built-in. There is also another way in which sociological laws are self-confirming: by taking one factor in history as basic, all the others can be reduced to conditions in which it operates. Thus if different responses occur in economically identical circumstances, the primacy of the economic factor is maintained by making the factors which produce the aberration into conditions, on which the economic factor acts as a prime cause. Again, a general system of sociology differs in one fundamental respect from every recognised science. The natural sciences depend on the possibility of abstracting and isolating their data from the total world of experience; sociology professes to apply to society as a whole, that is, to a universe, incapable of isolation, from which nothing can be excluded.

In practice, general social laws turn out to be one of three things. If they are not dogmatic assertions about the course of history, they are either platitudes, or else, to be made to fit the facts, they have to be subjected to more and more qualifications until in the end they are

[1] K. Popper, *The Poverty of Historicism* (1957), pp. 108-9.

applicable only to a single case. General sociology is thus no answer to the need for some theoretical element, other than inherited stereotypes, in our history.

CHAPTER III

THE PROBLEM OF SOCIAL HISTORY

IT might seem that we are now thrown back on what may be called naïve history—on the belief that the facts will speak for themselves, and presumably even select themselves, that all historical events are unique, and that generalisation is the crime against history. Of course, this belief is nonsense. All coherent thought requires general ideas: classificatory terms are necessary for rational discourse. A unique event could only be a miracle. Historical research begins with the discovery of 'facts' it is true, but, to be understood, these require to be given some meaning, just as do the facts that impinge on us, or that we observe, in everyday life. The task of reacting to common experience provides us with a set of rough concepts for dealing with these, and naïve history gets little farther.

A more sophisticated kind of history calls for a more sophisticated analysis. This is not to say that it needs a general theory, but it does need a language. In some respects it already has this. Thus, most of the history that has been written is political history, and since a long series of political scientists, from the time of Aristotle to the present day, have analysed political structures and events, there is no lack of a coherent and comprehensible political vocabulary, though even this requires to be continually redefined and brought into relation with new usages and changing political conditions. The language of economics was a much later invention. It did not exist when Hobbes, wanting to describe what we would call consumption and production, had to entitle his chapter 'Of the Nutrition and Procreation of a Commonwealth'. Now, however, economic history has a precise and carefully analysed set of terms, and this, I suggest, is one reason for the high standard it has achieved.

With these considerations we approach the crux of this discussion and begin to envisage the possibility of stating in more specific terms the problem of the relation of sociology and history. In the first place, the desire for a general sociological theory, applicable to the whole course of human existence, must, I have suggested, be dismissed as incompatible with critical history. What is needed, at least in the first place, is a set of concepts. It may be asked why the political and economic terms which we already have are not sufficient for this purpose. The answer is that there is now a desire for something more than political or economic history. If we are still far from clear what is meant by social history, this may not be unconnected with the fact that we still lack not only a workable vocabulary, but even the principles on which to build one. So far the tendency has been to rely on the terms provided by general sociological theory. This has led to an increasing tension between the theoretical pattern assumed in the language and the actual evidence discovered by historical research: alternatively, history written under the influence of sociological theory becomes a work of supererogation, since the theory has predetermined what the history will be. On the other hand, naïve, untheoretical history is reduced to attempting to employ for historical purposes the common language of the present day, regardless of fundamental changes in ideas and institutions: this is equally unsatisfactory.

If there is a way of escape from this dilemma it must be by abandoning both positions and trying to find some other solution. Here, I think, it is relevant to suggest that the historian does not normally solve his problems by abstract argument but does so in the process of dealing with actual difficulties presented by specific periods or subjects. The problem of social history appears, I believe, in one of its most crucial aspects in the history of the French Revolution, and a great deal, perhaps most, of the history of the French Revolution that is being written, or has been written for some time past, may be called social history in one sense or another. It therefore provides a valuable field for examining the problems of writing social history. One of the chief of these, the difficulty of terminology, can be illustrated by a brief essay in semantics, which may also serve as an explanation why the ordinary terms of contemporary society cannot provide the historian's social vocabulary.

Since society changes, while words remain, the relevance of terms of social description can alter radically. Thus, in eighteenth-century France a *manufacturier* was one who manufactured products with his hands, a *laboureur* was a fairly substantial peasant proprietor, and a *fermier* primarily anyone who paid a rent for property or position. None of these terms would convey the same meaning today. Not only at different times, but also in different countries the same word can have very different meanings, as for example the French *fermier* and the English farmer. Again, the French *paysan* is one who lives in and earns his living out of the country as opposed to the town, whatever his economic status; he is not necessarily, as in the English idea of the peasant, one of the poorer cultivators or a small-holder. A more important, indeed a major, source of confusion, is the fact that the social structures of two countries such as England and France have been for centuries so different that the terms employed in one, although often carried over to the other, are usually inapplicable. The English aristocracy did not correspond to the French noblesse, nor the English peer to the French *pair*. The bourgeoisie was not the same as the middle class. The French *officier* had no English equivalent, and the French *ordre* or estate no real parallel in England. The English class structure in the eighteenth century had more differences from than similarities with the social pattern of France; just as the European idea of class is now something of an alien term in present-day American social vocabulary.

The idea of class introduces another difficulty: there is a strong subjective element in all social descriptions. Who is, and who is not, middle-class today? Not everyone in eighteenth-century France who is down on the lists as a lawyer—*avocat*—had anything in practice to do with the law. During the revolution many a well-to-do employer appeared on official lists as a worker—*ouvrier*, and a landowner as a *cultivateur*. On the other hand, the secret agent, Noël Prigent, who described himself to the English as *négociant*, was said by his contemptuous fellow-Malouins to have earned his living selling fruit in the streets of St Malo.[1] A *négociant* usually meant someone engaged in substantial commerce, whereas *marchand* was the most indeterminate of descriptions. The small country towns or villages of France produced innumerable *marchands*, who represented merely the higher level of the rural artisanate.[2]

The same word could have a variety of meanings at the same time. As I have said, the eighteenth-century *fermier* was one who paid rent. Excluding the use of the term in the realm of finance, as the *fermiers généraux*, and confining ourselves to its use in the countryside, a *fermier* might be a steward or agent, who paid a fixed sum for the right of collecting rents or dues and made what he could out of them, or he might be one of the tenant farmers who rented land. Since the latter often worked fairly large farms, they could be equated with the better-off peasant proprietor—the *laboureur*, who might himself sometimes be a tenant, or *fermier*, for part of the land he cultivated. Hence, when a man is described as a *fermier* or a *laboureur*, it really tells us nothing except that he has an area of land above a certain size to cultivate. He might also be described as a *paysan*, which would tell us even less.

A word such as *métayer*, like the large social group which it described, has no English equivalent. This does not mean that it presents no problems. Indeed, I suspect that it reveals yet another source of confusion—that the same term may have very different meanings at the same time

---

[1] A. Cobban, 'The Beginning of the Channel Isles Correspondence 1789–1794', *English Historical Review*, LXXVII (1962), p. 47 and n. 5.

[2] *Cf.* Paul Bois, *Paysans de l'Ouest* (1960), p. 473.

in different parts of the same country. The generally accepted picture of the *métayer*, as we find him, for example, in Arthur Young, who was an acute and reliable observer, is of a poverty-stricken tenant of a small-holding, with a short three-, six- or nine-year lease, hiring the equipment and stock as well as the land, and paying for it partly, if not wholly, in kind. Western France in particular, according to Sée and Lefebvre, was dominated by this type of land tenure. A more recent historian has suggested that, at least in one district, this whole picture is based on a misunderstanding of the word *métairie*. In the Maine, and in the West generally, says M. Paul Bois, it refers not to the system of letting but to the size of the holding. In Maine and Anjou there were two main types of tenure, the *métairie* and the *bordage* (or *closerie*). The former, unexpectedly, proves to be the larger farm, sometimes of even 50 hectares, and the *métayer* is therefore equivalent to a *laboureur* or *fermier*, while the *bordage* was a small-holding of 3 to 10 hectares, cultivated by hand and not by the plough, except when one could be borrowed or hired.[1]

Many more examples of the difficulties of terminology might be given, but these should be enough to illustrate the scope of the problem. If this has generally not been adequately appreciated, it is, I believe, partly because the complexity of French society of the *ancien régime*, which is revealed by a detailed social analysis, has been concealed by the use of broad omnibus terms, such as bourgeois, *paysan*, noblesse. By and large, the legal division into orders—clergy, noblesse and third estate—has in the past

[1] *Op. cit.*, pp. 431–2.

provided the pattern for social historians, although in practice this legal classification had long before 1789 ceased to bear any close relation to social realities. To appreciate a man's real position in French society it would have been necessary to know, as well as his legal status, also his actual economic functions, the sources and extent of his wealth, his mode of life, his profession or office, his family, and during the revolution even his political affiliations. His rank on one scale might be very different from that on another. To add a final complication, the man who fell only into a single category was by no means the rule, and might even have been the exception. The peasant proprietor could also be a tenant farmer for part of his land, a merchant when he bought and sold produce, or a wage-earner when he worked on someone else's land. A lawyer might also be an estate manager and a merchant; he might also be a land-owner, for most persons of any social standing probably owned at least some land in town or country. In rural areas the small-holders and the rural artisanate might be quite distinct or might overlap. A noble could be a local official or a judge, an army officer, an ecclesiastic, a great landed proprietor or a working small-holder.

Amid the shifting sands of an uncertain and uncritical social terminology, the historian of eighteenth-century France has too often been content with broad generalisations possessing even at the time only a very rough relation to social realities, and now distorted by all the overtones of nineteenth-century sociological thought and present-day social conditions. The first necessity for writing the social history of the revolution is therefore to abandon the existing terminology. This is far from being a mere negative requirement. It is indeed a revolutionary step, for this terminology, with all its defects, embodies, as will be seen, a specific theory of the revolution, and to abandon the language is to abandon the theory.

Adequately to deal with the social history of the revolution, an empirical examination of social facts is needed, such as a contemporary sociologist would make of his own society. An estimate of social position must not be based on a single criterion, legal, political or economic, as it often has been in the past, but on a plurality of tests— actual wealth and its nature, sources of income, social status and prestige, origin and direction of social movement of the individual and his family, legal order, political orientation, contemporary esteem, economic function, personal aspirations and grievances, and so on.

Not only the social classification but also the nature and direction of social movement in history needs to be considered afresh. The whole conception of rising and falling classes, which is closely involved with the idea of revolution, is in need of revision. The movement of individuals from one class to another, if on a sufficiently large scale, has been equated with the rise or fall of a class. This is clearly unsound. However many sons of peasants, say, move into the town and become lawyers or merchants, this cannot be called the rise of the peasantry. A class has been compared to a hotel, which remains the same though a continually changing clientele passes through it.[1] A class rises, properly speaking, when it acquires political power and increased economic well-being and yet re-

[1] Schlumpeter, *op. cit.*, p. 126.

22

mains the same class. Put in this way, the 'rise of the bourgeoisie' in the French Revolution ceases to be a platitude and becomes a problem.

The essential thing is that we shall cease to take theories for facts. The distinguished French historian, M. Albert Soboul, almost in the same breath tells us that the triumph of the bourgeoisie is the essential fact of the revolution, and that we have no history of the bourgeoisie during the revolution.[1] In other words, what he calls the essential fact is no more than an act of faith. We will have to choose whether we will believe M. Soboul when, as a theorist, he tells us that he knows for certain what the revolution was, or when, as an historian, he admits that only after many local and regional social studies have been made will works of synthesis on the different classes and social categories be possible.[2] Of course, even while assuming that he knew in advance essentially what will be discovered, it was a step forward to recognise that the research which should demonstrate it has not yet been done. I believe that we can go a little farther than this, and that quite a lot in fact has been done. If it has only very partially been used by historians, this is because much of it does not fit conveniently into the accepted theory. In this study, therefore, I do not propose to begin with any kind of theoretical discussion. The weakness of much social thought, it seems to me, is that it is so largely concerned with packing its bag (or even with working out a general theory about the way in which a bag should be packed) for a journey which is never taken. I shall try

[1] A. Soboul, *Précis*, p. 11.
[2] *Ibid.*

to avoid this danger by treating the problem of the social interpretation of the French Revolution as a series of specific historical problems, and ask such questions as: what are the facts of the so-called bourgeois revolution, and in particular who were the bourgeois? What was the feudalism which they are supposed to have overthrown? How was the bourgeois revolution related to the revolt of the peasantry? This raises the problem of the relation-ship of town and country. Again, what part was played in the revolutionary situation by the lower social elements? This broadly raises the problem of the relation of rich and poor. Above all, my aim will be to try to get away from the traditional sociological clichés and to break down the large omnibus classes which are calculated to accept practically any passenger who can pay a minimum set fare, regardless of where he gets on or gets off or what may be his real station in life, and to substitute for them social distinctions and classifications based on historical actualities.

CHAPTER IV

THE MEANING OF FEUDALISM

As every schoolboy knows, the perfect cliché for any period in history since the expulsion from the Garden of Eden is the rise of the middle classes; and all orthodox histories of the French Revolution assume that this was the period when they completed their rise and finally overthrew feudalism. Behind this theory is the assumption that social history can be divided into a few large and homogeneous phases, which are repeated in the same order and the same shape by all societies. Within this general pattern, feudalism is taken to extend in European history from the early Middle Ages to its overthrow by the bourgeois revolution, which occurred in England in the seventeenth century, in France in the eighteenth, and in most of the rest of Europe in the course of the nineteenth and twentieth centuries.

All this assumes, of course, that we know what we mean by feudalism. Medieval historians, who ought to be able to tell us about this, seem to have doubts. They stress the different meaning of the term in different countries,[1] and protest against its use to describe conditions in eighteenth-century France.[2] One of the chief

[1] M. Reinhard, 'Sur l'histoire de la Révolution française', *Annales* (1959), p. 568.

[2] *Ibid.*, p. 569.

authorities on feudalism enjoins us to employ the word with caution. The word *féodalité*, writes Professor Ganshof, 'lends itself to confusion'.[1] *'Féodo-vassalique'* institutions, he says, ceased to be an historically truly essential characteristic of the political system or social structure in Western Europe from the end of the thirteenth century.[2] By 1789, he concludes, the word had become a mere bogey, a term of abuse like 'fanaticism', and with as little precise content.[3] Francis Bacon saw the same disappearance of meaning, along with the retention of terms, when he discussed the legal survival in sixteenth-century England of the names of military tenures which had entirely ceased to fulfil their original function. *'Vocabula manent'*, he wrote, *'res fugiunt.'* The term 'fiscal feudalism' has been employed to describe the anachronistic survival into Tudor and Stuart times of such medieval rights as wardship and marriage, which had by then largely come to be a financial expedient concentrated in the hands of the Crown and used mainly for raising revenue or rewarding royal officials or favourites.[4]

It must not be supposed, however, that historians invented the belief in eighteenth-century France that feudalism was the enemy. There can be no doubt that there was a widespread attack on something that was called feudalism, and that this attack was the expression of deeply-felt grievances. The problem is to identify these grievances and discover what, if anything, was feudal about them.

[1] F. L. Ganshof, *Qu'est ce que la féodalité?* (1947), p. 11.
[2] *Ibid.*   [3] *Ibid.*
[4] J. Hurstfield, 'The Profits of Fiscal Feudalism, 1541–1602', *Economic History Review*, VIII (1955–56), pp. 53–61.

It is reasonable to raise this question, because the revolutionaries had considerable doubts on the subject themselves. The Constituent Assembly, when it resolved to abolish feudal rights, found that it did not really know, and certainly was not agreed on, what were feudal and what were non-feudal among the various rights. The legislation of 4–11 August having in its first article 'entirely destroyed' the so-called feudal rights, in its subsequent ones partially restored them. The Feudal Committee tried to draw a line between *droits personnels* and *droits réels*, but this was a distinction derived from Roman Law and inappropriate to the extraordinary variety of seigniorial rights. Compromises favourable to the *seigneurs* were naturally those adopted by an Assembly and a Committee composed in large part of *seigneurs*, say the editors of the papers of the Committee.[1] This was a practical as well as a legal problem. Its historic origins are easy to detect. Land changed hands rapidly in the later Middle Ages, passing from the possession of nobles into that of *roturiers*; but though the latter might acquire the land, they could not exercise the rights of a feudal lord over it. To cope with this difficulty, sixteenth-century jurists employed a distinction between *domaine direct*, which always remained in the hands of the *seigneur*, and *domaine utile*, which could be alienated. By the eighteenth century, *domaine utile* had come to be regarded as the true property right, and *domaine direct* as a sort of 'servitude' on it.[2] The eighteenth-century jurist, R. J. Pothier, put

[1] Ph. Sagnac et P. Caron, *Les comités des droits féodaux et de législation et l'abolition du régime seigneurial (1789–1793)* (1907), pp. xi–xiii.
[2] G. Lizerand, *Le régime rural de l'ancienne France* (1942), p. 85.

the situation thus: 'He who has *domaine utile* is called proprietor or *seigneur utile*, he who has *domaine direct* is called simply *seigneur*. He is indeed the proprietor of his right of *seigneurie*, but it is not he, it is the *seigneur utile*, who is properly the owner of the property.'[1] In other words, by the eighteenth century, as Marc Bloch says, the tenant was the real proprietor, and he is called so in the *terriers*.[2]

This does not end the story. Seigniorial rights also became alienable, and as they began to pass into non-noble hands, *roturiers* came to exercise rights of *seigneurie*. Thus the ownership both of land and of seigniorial rights became separable from noblesse as a personal quality. An official reply to a query on the conditions of admissibility to electoral assemblies of the noblesse in 1789 was that the possession of a fief did not confer the quality of noblesse. Finally, even descent or occupation came to be insecure tests of noble status. In the later Middle Ages and the early modern period, the noblesse had been recruited by a massive entry of the *bourgeoisie d'office*.[3] This did not prevent a reverse movement of nobles into remunerative offices in the eighteenth century. 'I have seen in my youth', writes Duclos, 'the low offices of finance as the reward of lacqueys. Today one finds more nobles in them than *roturiers*.'[4]

Nobles were also moving downwards in a less reward-ing way. Perhaps there might be postulated a social law,

---

[1] Cited in M. Garaud, *La Révolution et la propriété foncière* (1959), p. 1.
[2] M. Bloch, *Les caractères originaux de l'histoire rurale française* (1931), p. 134.
[3] *Ibid.*, p. 138.
[4] Cited in H. Thirria, *La vie privée des financiers au XVIIIe siècle* (1895), p. 107.

which would be as good as most other social laws, of the conservation of classes, by which when some members of them are falling out of them others are rising into them. The picture of the country noble, the *hobereau*, in Chateaubriand's *Mémoires d'outre tombe*, though sentimentalised, is a version of reality. The popular saying—'He's a gentleman of Beauce, who stays in bed when his breeches are mended'—cuts closer to the bone. In Brittany nobles are found as steward, gamekeeper, wig-maker, chairman, muleteer.[1] In Normandy nobles were in the *dépôts de mendicité*.[2] The father of the diamond-necklace heroine, Jeanne de Valois de Rémy de St Luz, all his family estates gone, lived in a corner of his broken-down château with a peasant woman, who ran away with a soldier while the count went to die in the pauper hospital of La Samaritaine at Paris. Yet Mme de la Motte justly claimed to be descended from Henry II of France. To the election of 1789 in Poitou seven nobles came dressed as peasants. They were lent swords and their expenses at the inn were paid for them.[3] The noblesse of Blois, in their *cahier*, pleaded for that section of their order which was confined by its poverty to a rural existence—its life, they said, dramatically if not wholly accurately, divided between digging the fields and defending the state.[4] Barbier, in 1751, described the provinces as filled with nobles who were burdened with children they could not,

---

[1] H. Carré, *La Noblesse de France et l'opinion publique au XVIIIe siècle* (1920) pp. 130–1.
[2] *Ibid.*
[3] *Ibid.*
[4] F. Grille, *Introduction aux Mémoires sur la Révolution française* (1825), II, pp. 312–13.

afford to educate: their sons passed their youth amid the peasants, 'in ignorance and boorishness'.[1] Revolutionary propagandists themselves bore witness to the existence of great divisions within the noblesse, by attempting to exploit them and appeal to the poor nobles—'this numerous class of gentlemen peasants, restricted by a gothic prejudice to a single form of livelihood', to quote Brissot's *Patriote française* in 1790—against the aristocracy of the Court.[2]

At the opposite extreme were the great nobles whose debts were often only the measure of their wealth in land, investments, or pensions and places. There was also a considerable body of what one might almost call middle-class nobles. A guess might be made that it was this group which survived the revolution most successfully. In many towns there were reasonably well-to-do nobles not easily distinguishable from the prosperous bourgeois. In the city of Toulouse it was such nobles who paid by far the highest taxes,[3] which incidentally damages another cliché. The income of the average noble at Toulouse was two or three times that of the successful merchant or lawyer.[4] Perhaps their prosperity here, as well as the efficient management of their estates[5] which helps to account for it, may not be unconnected with the comparatively recent emergence of the Toulousain nobility from the world of business or finance. Thus, the tax-

---

[1] Cited in Carré, *La Noblesse de France*, p. 123.

[2] *Ibid.*

[3] J. Sentou, 'Impôts et citoyens actifs à Toulouse au début de la Révolution', *Annales du Midi*, LXI (1948), p. 179.

[4] R. Forster, *The Nobility of Toulouse in the eighteenth century* (1960), p. 175; *cf.* Sentou, *loc. cit.*

[5] Forster, p. 38.

farmer Jacob, at the end of the seventeenth century, bought a seigniorial fief. The family married above them, changed their name and by 1760 were barons. Again, the merchant Picot was ennobled by municipal office, the *capitoulat*, in 1738, and his son voted with the noblesse in 1789.[1]

The wealth, status and social origins of the local noblesse evidently varied enormously from one part of France to another. Nowhere was there more social equality, says Mercier, than in Paris.[2] The number of nobles in the capital cannot be estimated, but about 1,000 attended the electoral assemblies of 1789.[3] The unexpected phenomenon here is the repeated attempts of the noblesse to claim the status of bourgeois and their complaints at being separated from the *tiers état*.[4] A *conseiller* of the Parlement of Paris declared, 'There is no noble, whatever his rank, who is not accustomed to hear himself called Bourgeois of Paris, and there is none who could be offended to find himself sitting beside a member of the *tiers état* judged worthy of its confidence.'[5] At the assembly of the *tiers état* of *Paris hors les murs*, the first representative of the *bailliage* of Versailles, a noble, declared that he believed he had a right to sit in the *tiers état* 'because he was in commerce and all of his family had presented themselves in that Order, that one of his relations had even been elected deputy by the Assembly of

[1] *Ibid.*, pp. 25–6.
[2] L. S. Mercier, *Tableau de Paris*.
[3] C. L. Chassin, *Les Élections et les cahiers de Paris en 1789* (1888–89), II, p. 217.
[4] *Ibid.*, I, pp. 92–3, 255; II, pp. 218–19, 257.
[5] *Ibid.*, I, p. 360.

the Commons of Rouen, although a noble in the same degree as himself', adding that he had not bought noblesse, but his ancestors had obtained it for services rendered to the state, and that he had always remained in commerce.[1]

This attitude on the part of the noblesse of Paris was by no means to the satisfaction of all members of the Order. It was attacked by a 'provincial gentleman', who asserted against them the importance of the distinction of Orders. The coterie of signatories of the *Mémoirs des Princes* also expressed its disapproval.[2] The *tiers état* of Paris on the other hand, in their session of 26 April, discussing 'whether the nobles should be made to withdraw', observed that it was necessary to distinguish between different kinds of noblesse, and not to confuse those who had bought it with merchants to whom it had been accorded in recognition of the services they had rendered to the state in commerce, or as municipal officers. Both the latter, it was decided, might be considered as belonging to the *tiers état* and allowed to remain in its assemblies.[3]

Among the various types of noble, representing all levels of wealth and poverty, with widely divergent sources of income and social status, there was little or no unity. In this situation, to attack nobility as a personal state was partly to attack a phantom. True, it *was* attacked, but I hope to show later that other sources of enmity had to be added to make the noble an object of hostility.[4] All that need be argued here is that the attack on feudalism

[1] *Ibid.*, IV, p. 163.
[2] *Ibid.*, II, p. 252.
[3] *Ibid.*, III, p. 30.
[4] *Cf. infra*, pp. 82–3.

cannot be equated with a simple attack on the nobles as such.

What was the object of attack then? A general opinion, which is endorsed by Professor Reinhard, is that it was the *droits seigneuriaux*.[1] I have already suggested that to describe these payments in money and kind, or services, as still 'feudal' in the eighteenth century is to stretch the meaning of the term to a point at which it loses all historical meaning. There are other difficulties as well. The incidence of seigniorial rights varied greatly from province to province. They seem to have been comparatively unimportant in parts of Maine,[2] in Alsace,[3] Anjou, Bordelais, Guyenne.[4] In the *cahiers* of the *département* of the Sarthe the peasants did not attack, or even—except rarely —use the term, *droits féodaux*. They criticised separate, specific dues, but even in this respect only 20 parishes out of 300 asked for their suppression without compensation.[5] The *cahiers* of Neubourg in Normandy complained of the *taille* but not of the seigniorial system.[6] Perhaps this is why, in the rural troubles of 1789, the *seigneur* of Neubourg was undisturbed.[7] The marquis de Ferrières, deputy for the noblesse of Saumur in 1789, rode out the revolution without suffering attack though not without some alarms. Like many another noble, he escaped prescription and stayed quietly and undisturbed in his château.[8]

---

[1] Reinhard, 'Sur l'histoire de la Révolution française', p. 557.

[2] *Ibid.*, p. 558.

[3] R. Dufraisse, *Paysans et forêts sous la Révolution: les droits d'usage* (1959).

[4] M. Garaud, *La Révolution et la propriété foncière*, pp. 170–1.

[5] Bois, *Paysans de l'Ouest*, pp. 710–11.

[6] A. Plaisse, *La baronnie de Neubourg* (1961), p. 594.

[7] *Ibid.*, p. 622.

[8] *Cf.* Ferrières, marquis de, *Correspondance inédite 1789, 1790, 1791*, ed. H. Carré (1932); *cf.* Lefebvre, *Études*, p. 280, where it is pointed out that this was the case of many nobles.

These, of course, are only random examples. It would be equally possible, by choosing other, and perhaps better known ones, to draw a picture in other parts of France of a major peasant offensive against seigniorial rights. This was none the less widespread for not always taking a violent form. The *ancien régime* had trained the peasantry in litigiousness, and peasants suspicious of the legality of seigniorial titles, and doubtful of the honesty of the *terriers* in which they were registered, often tested them in the law courts. The *tiers* of the *bailliage* of Saint-Omer called for the abandonment of the legal maxim *nulle terre sans seigneur* and the substitution of that of *nul seigneur sans titre*.[1] Another *cahier* of the Pas-de-Calais insisted that no *terrier* should be drawn up without authorisation from the Crown or from a sovereign court, and without public notice given four times in four successive fortnights.[2] Doubtless the renewal of *terriers* was commonly used as a means of reviving or increasing seigniorial payments, though even the reasonable assumption that the peasants were always opposed to this measure is not a safe one. In a *cahier* of Autun they complained that the *terrier* was so old that they did not know what they owed, and petitioned the king for permission to call on their *seigneur* to renew it.[3]

Whatever qualifications or limitations we have to introduce, however, the close association, almost equal to an identification, between the attack on seigniorial rights

[1] H. Loriquet (ed.), *Cahiers de doléances de 1789 dans le département du Pas-de-Calais* (1891), I, pp. 121, 564.

[2] *Ibid.*, I, pp. 448–9.

[3] C. A. Desplaces de Charmasse, *Cahiers des paroisses et communautés du bailliage d'Autun* (1874), p. 150.

and the attack on 'feudalism' must remain the basic fact on which all discussion of the latter must centre. If 'feudalism' in 1789 did not mean seigniorial rights, it meant nothing. To these we must therefore turn our attention.

CHAPTER V

THE ATTACK ON SEIGNIORIAL RIGHTS

CONTEMPORARY references can be found in the eighteenth century for the view that seigniorial rights and dues were largely obsolete in practice. In 1735 d'Argenson wrote, 'There only remains the shadow of the *seigneurie*', and rather later Letrône, 'There is nothing real in feudalism except the expenses, that is to say there is no profit except for the agents and the compilers of *terriers*'. But they cancel this out themselves when Letrône goes on to call it 'a social evil', and d'Argenson adds, 'all the same it is annoying and harmful'.[1] Seigniorial rights certainly survived, even if not as universally as has sometimes been supposed, and they were an object of widespread attack; but is this attack correctly described as the struggle of the bourgeois against feudalism? I have already suggested that the equation of the system of seigniorial rights with feudalism is historically unjustifiable, but this can be disregarded for the moment, as a matter of terminology, though it is rather more than that: M. Méthivier, following other French historians, has rightly protested against the confusion of feudal and seigniorial.[2] There is a problem involved, however, which is a matter of historical fact. Is the identification of

[1] H. Doniol, *La Révolution française et la féodalité* (1874), pp. 21–2.
[2] H. Méthivier, *L'ancien régime* (1961), p. 18.

the bourgeois as the social force responsible for the attack on seigniorial rights a valid one?

This is not a new doubt. Georges Lefebvre pointed out that, up to 14 July 1789, the bourgeois had neither the desire nor the intention to attack the seigniorial rights,[1] and that they had no idea of calling on the peasants to revolt, or of abolishing seigniorial rights without compensation.[2] It was observed long ago that the abolition of seigniorial rights was not among the articles of which the *bailliage cahiers* demanded immediate adoption, or, if they did, only in districts where towns were rare, or had little preponderance, as in Brittany.[3] There is no lack of evidence to support this view. Only a few examples need be given. The *cahier* of Reims ignores the whole subject,[4] as does that of Rouen.[5] The peasants of Neubourg in Normandy complain of the *taille* but not of the seigniorial régime.[6] Normandy may have been an exceptional area, in which seigniorial rights were of only slight importance. Another example is provided by the *bailliage* of Mirecourt in Lorraine. Here the original *cahier* of the town makes no mention of seigniorial rights; on the other hand, the rural *cahiers* are full of protests and demands for their suppression, sometimes with, and sometimes without, compensation. In the final *cahier*, drawn up for the whole

[1] Lefebvre, *Études*, p. 249.

[2] *Ibid.*, p. 258.

[3] E. Champion, *La France d'après les cahiers de 1789* (1921), p. 95.

[4] G. Laurent, *Reims et la région rémoise à la veille de la Révolution: la convocation des États généraux de 1789. Introduction aux cahiers de doléances du bailliage de Reims* (1930), p. 242.

[5] M. Bouloiseau (ed.), *Cahiers de doléances du tiers état du bailliage de Rouen* (1957), I, p. cxii.

[6] Plaisse, *La baronnie de Neubourg*, p. 594.

bailliage, it was evidently impossible to ignore the subject entirely, but the townsmen, whose influence was dominant in the *bailliage cahier*, shuffled out of what seems to have been a difficulty for them by saying that they thought the *États généraux* would probably not be interested in the matter.[1] Where the *cahiers* of the *bailliages* do recognise the need for something to be done about seigniorial dues, they most often moderate the demand by putting the abolition in terms of *rachat*—abolition only in return for a purchase price. As the *cahier* of Autun declared, 'In abolishing these servitudes, the *seigneurs* should not be victimised'.[2]

A further indication of the attitude of the towns is to be found in the fact that there was one seigniorial right, if it can be called such, which they commonly opposed. But this was franc-fief, and it was a payment not to the *seigneur* but to the crown, due after land that was part of a fief passed from noble into non-noble possession. The motive for demanding its abolition was frankly expressed by the *tiers état* of Rouen, which said that franc-fief harmed the sale of property.[3] The *cahiers* of Walloon Flanders complained that by hindering *roturiers* from buying fiefs it lowered their value; the nobles of the *bailliage* of Lille called for its abolition on property under 100,000 livres in value.[4]

Apart from franc-fief, the *cahiers* of the towns are conspicuously reluctant to suggest that anything should be done about seigniorial dues. Nevertheless it is true that

[1] E. Martin, *Cahiers de doléances du bailliage de Mirecourt* (1928), p. 254.
[2] Desplaces de Charmasse, *Cahiers d'Autun*, p. 107.
[3] Bouloiseau, *Cahiers de Rouen*, I, p. 237.
[4] G. Lefebvre, *Paysans du Nord* (1924), p. 138.

the National Assembly did take the decisive step towards their abolition. This must be accounted for somehow. There is no difficulty in doing so. It is accepted by practically all recent historians of the revolution that what forced the National Assembly into the decisions of the night of the fourth of August was the widespread and alarming peasant revolt of the spring and early summer of 1789. The view once held that the fourth of August represented a spontaneous outburst of idealism on the part of an assembly of nobles, clergy and bourgeois, anxious to relieve an oppressed peasantry from its burdens, has not survived a closer examination of what actually happened. A number of the more liberal, but also more realistic, members of the Assembly had come to the conclusion, almost certainly a correct one, that unless concessions were made to the peasantry the whole of rural France would remain in a state of endemic rebellion. The generous gestures of 4 August were contrived in advance, and planned for a night session in the hope that many who might have resisted them would be absent. True, a wave of emotion swept the members present and many more sacrifices than had probably been intended were spontaneously announced, but there were second thoughts during the following seven days, from 4 to 11 August, when the principles proclaimed in the enthusiasm of the first night were given specific form. It was in these discussions, and the consequent legislation, that the intention of abolishing feudalism was particularly emphasised; but it was for the purpose not of extending but of limiting the scope of the changes.

The Assembly based its final legislation on the distinction

between feudal and non-feudal property. In fact this was almost an impossible distinction to make. The confusion of the two had been facilitated by legal fictions. For example, when a *seigneur* in the Nord sold the right of *terrage* (a payment, or *cens*, on the harvest, but attached to the land and not the type of product), without specifying that he was also alienating the *directe*, or seigniorial title, in the hands of the new proprietor it was held to become a simple land rent.[1]

Another illustration of the difficulty of distinguishing between feudal privilege and property rights is provided by the case of seigniorial pews in churches. These would seem as clear a case of mere privilege as one could hope to find; but petitions to the Feudal Committee show that the matter was not always so simple. Thus the directory of the *département* of Finistère explains that in 1741 the church of Saint-Louis at Brest was presented with four marble columns. In 1751 the sons of the donor paid for the columns to be carved, on condition that a pew should remain in their family in perpetuity. The confiscation of this pew, says the directory, is a violation of the right of property. Either it should be restored, or at least the 2,500 livres paid for carving the columns should be given back, since the columns themselves cannot be.[2]

In August 1791 a citizen of Caussade in Lot explains that he formerly possessed the right to a pew in the church, which he had sold in 1776. The purchaser, who had now been summoned to give it up, was demanding a return of the 400 livres purchase price. The petitioner asks

[1] *Ibid.*, pp. 140-1.
[2] Sagnac et Caron, *Les comités des droits féodaux*, pp. 194-5.

for an opinion on this demand.[1] From Carcassonne came the suggestion, in April 1790, that pew rights should be abolished where they were based solely on seigniorial right, but preserved for those who had obtained them by founding chapels, or making considerable repairs or improvements in the church fabric, so long as their contributions constituted a capital sum sufficient to furnish an income equal to the annual rent of a pew.[2]

The attempt to draw a distinction between payments and services which were feudal and those which were non-feudal and so susceptible of being adjudged strictly as property rights was unrealistic at a time when for centuries they had been subject to sale and purchase. It was used by the Assembly in an attempt to save what could be saved from the wreck of seigniorial fortunes, and a good deal would have been saved if the Assembly had been able to achieve its aim. The Feudal Commission, given the task of putting the legislation of 4–11 August into practice, took the view that was favourable to the owner of seigniorial rights whenever possible. Thus it decided that *mainmorte réelle* could be considered as a payment by the freed serf in return for the concession of land to him, and hence as a contractual property right and not a feudal payment.[3] It adopted the interpretation of *triage* most favourable to the *seigneur*. The Committee, replying to a question on 22 September 1791, ruled that a ci-devant *seigneur* was to be maintained in his rights unless and until it was clearly proved that their possession did not derive from an original grant of land.[4]

---

[1] *Ibid.*, p. 196. [2] *Ibid.*, pp. 186–7.
[3] *Ibid.*, p. xiii. [4] *Ibid.*, pp. 170–1.

The eminent feudal lawyer Merlin de Douai, reporting to the Assembly on behalf of the Committee on 8 February 1790, practically admitted that its aim was to consolidate the former dues under a new name. 'In destroying the feudal régime', he told the Assembly, 'you did not mean to despoil the legitimate proprietors of fiefs of their possessions, but you changed the nature of these properties. Freed henceforth from the laws of feudalism, they remain subject to those of landed estate; in a word, they have ceased to be fiefs and have become true freeholds (*alleux*). . . . There are no more fiefs; hence all the actual dues (*droits utiles*) with which the formerly feudal property is burdened should no longer be considered as anything but purely property rights.'[1]

The aims of the National Assembly, and of its Feudal Committee, are hardly in doubt. How far they were able to achieve them is another matter. What actually happened to the feudal dues in the first years of the revolution is still in dispute. Did the peasants stop paying their dues at once, whether they had been legally pronounced feudal or not? For those which had been decreed purchasable was compensation paid, and if so for how long? These are questions to which we do not know the answer. Probably there is no answer, or rather there are too many, varying from district to district all over France. These temporary doubts and hesitations, reluctances and oppositions, do not affect the basic fact that in one way or another, quickly or slowly, legally or by usurpation, the seigniorial dues and rights disappeared.

The question that interests us here is not what hap-

[1] A. Aulard, *La Révolution française et le régime féodal* (1919), p. 109.

pened, which by and large is not in dispute, but why it happened in the way in which it did. That the peasantry, once they envisaged the possibility, should have fought for the abolition of seigniorial dues in every way in which they could, is easily to be understood. But if the 'abolition of feudalism by the bourgeoisie' means anything, as has been said above, it can only mean the abolition of seigniorial dues; and whatever we understand by the bourgeoisie—a point to which I must revert later—it must include the men who drew up the *cahiers* in the towns and the members of the *tiers état* in the National Assembly. The actual historical fact which needs to be explained, therefore, is not the supposed 'abolition of feudalism by the bourgeoisie', but on the contrary their opposition to its abolition—for there can be no doubt of their opposition to the abolition of the system of seigniorial dues and rights which represented what, if anything, was left of feudalism in 1789.

Was this reform—even if the leaders of the *tiers état* in the towns and the National Assembly accepted it under pressure—one which was contrary to their material interests? If this were so it would explain their attitude in 1789. This point deserves investigation. It has been suggested that by 1789 seigniorial rights had often passed out of the hands of nobles into those of *roturiers*.[1] The conquest of the land by non-nobles had already begun in the Middle Ages, and this included the acquisition of fiefs.[2] The process has been described as the decapitation of the

---

[1] Reinhard, 'Sur la Révolution française', p. 558.

[2] *Cf.* Plaisse, *La baronnie de Neubourg*, p. 352; G. Roupnel, *La ville et la campagne au XVIIe siècle: étude sur les populations du pays dijonnais* (1922, 2nd ed. 1952), p. 249; H. Méthivier, *L'ancien régime* (1961), p. 20.

commercial classes by the desire to own land.[1] It was facilitated by the inherent tendency of the nobles to accumulate debts and so to be forced to sell their lands or *seigneuries*. By the eighteenth century, says Georges Lefebvre, in Walloon Flanders seigniorial rights were as active a market as land.[2] Of course, some of the purchasers themselves became nobles in their turn; but by 1789 the *tiers état* included many owners of seigniorial rights.[3] Non-noble *seigneurs* are noted in Guyenne,[4] round Bordeaux,[5] Rouen,[6] Reims,[7] Valenciennes,[8] and doubtless far more examples could be collected.

A single case which is of interest in itself is that of the *seigneurie* of Villeneuve-de-Rivière in the *généralité* of Auch. Jean d'Estrémé, of the same village, bought the *seigneurie* in 1761. He was of peasant origin, but the family had acquired wealth in the wool trade and the trade of mules with Spain, and he is described as *négociant*. His history also illustrates another aspect of the situation. D'Estrémé seems to have been a regular village tyrant, greedy to gain all he could from his seigniorial rights, as well as to assert his rank as 'maître et seigneur'. He en-

---

[1] H. Hauser, 'The characteristic features of French Economic History from the Middle of the Sixteenth to the Middle of the Eighteenth Century', *Economic History Review*, IV (1933), p. 263. 'A constant haemorrhage of capital, which removed it from business as soon as it had been created; and the commercial class was decapitated by the transformation of its best representatives into professional men.'

[2] Lefebvre, *Paysans du Nord*, p. 161 n.

[3] Doniol, *La Révolution française et la féodalité*, pp. 27, 39.

[4] Garaud, *La Révolution et la propriété foncière*, p. 7.

[5] C. E. Labrousse, *La Crise de l'économie française à la fin de l'ancien régime et au début de la Révolution* (1944), p. 566.

[6] Bouloiseau, *Cahiers de Rouen*, I, p. xxx.

[7] Laurent, *Reims et la région rémoise*, p. 179.

[8] Lefebvre, *Paysans du Nord*, p. 15.

gaged in long lawsuits with the community over the forge and the mill, and took the cases right up to the Conseil du Roi, where the peasant opposition finally won, in 1787, on the eve of a greater victory.[1]

Again, the commune of La Capelle-Cabanac, in Lot, protested in January 1790 about a *seigneurie* sold in 1743 to one Jean-Baptiste Bonnamie Duroc, a *roturier*, who hastened to adopt the title of '*messire*', began lawsuits against the inhabitants to claim his dues, and forced the local consuls to wear hoods in his livery and take the oath to him bare-headed and on their knees. The petitioners add, as not irrelevant to decisions he obtained in his favour, the fact that his son was a *conseiller* in the *parlement* of Toulouse.[2]

A recent historian of the peasantry of Burgundy has described the investment of urban wealth in the country during the eighteenth century as a veritable 'capitalist offensive'. It destroyed, he says, the old village community and dealt a death blow to the former *seigneurie*.[3] The peasants complained that the good old *seigneurs* (doubtless greatly idealised in retrospect) had sold their lands and their *seigneuries* to bourgeois who were indifferent to the interests of the rural population.[4] It was even complained that the money of the bourgeois was more dangerous to the villagers than the obligations of *mainmorte*. In 1751, the intendant of Dijon, Joly de Fleury,

---

[1] C. Anglade, 'Un exemple de la réaction nobiliaire dans le Comminges à la veille de la Révolution', *Annales du Midi* (1953), pp. 171–80.

[2] Sagnac et Caron, *Les Comités des droits féodaux*, p. 83.

[3] P. de Saint-Jacob, *Les Paysans de la Bourgogne du Nord au dernier siècle de l'ancien régime* (1960), pp. 469, 472.

[4] *Ibid.*, p. 571.

wrote to Paris that where *mainmorte* survived outsiders could not buy up the lands of the villagers, but elsewhere bourgeois from the towns had become proprietors of all the land and reduced the inhabitants to the status of mere day-labourers.[1] Perhaps this was special pleading, but it sounds not implausible; and in this case the great campaign against *mainmorte* need not have been so purely inspired by humanitarian sentiments as we had supposed.

The rise of capitalist enterprise in the countryside drove the owners of *seigneuries* into a search for enhanced profits.[2] There are many indications that the new owners were determined to obtain the maximum return from their investment, and that their exactions were particularly feared by the peasantry.[3] It is customary, says the *cahier* of Albas in Cahors, for *parvenus* to abuse their authority.[4] It is not difficult to believe that this was true, but more to our purpose is the actual ownership of the rights, whether they were abused or not. To what extent, and subject to what local variations, the seigniorial rights had passed into non-noble possession, we cannot at present say; but that the movement had been on a considerable scale, and that it affected the attitude of the town middle classes to the question of their abolition, cannot reasonably be doubted.

The Russian historian, Porchnev, has described this process, the existence of which he implicitly admits, as the

[1] *Ibid.*, p. 423.

[2] *Ibid.*, p. 413.

[3] S. Herbert, *The Fall of Feudalism in France* (1921), pp. 43, 47; J. Savina et D. Bernard (eds.), *Cahiers de doléances des sénéchaussées de Quimper et de Concarneau*, I (1927), p. xv; G. Lizerand, *Le régime rural de l'ancienne France* (1942), p. 170; F. L. Ford, *Robe and Sword* (1953), pp. 165, 167; Garaud, *La Révolution et la propriété foncière*, pp. 171–2.

[4] V. Fourastié, *Cahiers de doléances de la sénéchaussée de Cahors* (1908), p. 4.

'feudalisation' of part of the bourgeoisie.[1] Lefebvre inter-
prets it in the same way, and argues that it caused the
bourgeois landed proprietors to identify their interests
with those of the feudal *seigneurs*.[2] Alternatively, it has
been described as the 'embourgeoisement' of the land,[3] and
Lefebvre seems to move a long way towards this latter
view when he allows that it was partly by way of the
seigniorial rights that capitalism entered agriculture.[4] The
two views are hardly reconcilable, and the latter, which
seems the more realistic, calls for closer examination.

To understand the problem presented by seigniorial
rights in the eighteenth century, their real nature must be
appreciated. It has been pointed out that a seigniorial
fortune was made up of a host of petty dues and claims,
some in money and some in kind or services, the effective
collection of which called for careful management. Many
of the nobles, unable to provide this, had tended to let
their petty seigniorial rights fall into disuse. *Seigneuries*, it
is said, only prospered in the hands of those with other
sources of revenue, who could invest their surplus profits
and their business experience in a fief.[5] In this respect, at
least, it is possible to describe the so-called 'feudal reaction' as less a reversion to the past than the application
to old relationships of new business techniques.[6]

Another way of coping with this problem was for the
seigneur, whether he was noble or not, to save himself the

[1] Cited in Méthivier, *L'ancien régime*, p. 76.
[2] Lefebvre, *Études*, pp. 166–7.
[3] Méthivier, *L'ancien régime*, p. 30.
[4] Lefebvre, *Études*, p. 636.
[5] Méthivier, *L'ancien régime*, p. 66.
[6] Ford, *Robe and Sword*, p. 167.

worry of management, and at the same time increase his revenue, by letting out the collection of his seigniorial rights to agents or *fermiers*.[1] This resulted in the rise of a large body of intermediaries—office holders, seigniorial judges, *procureurs*, notaries, lawyers of various kinds—and a lesser world of clerks, collectors, *feudistes* to draw up *terriers*, and so on, all with a material interest in the system of seigniorial dues.[2] Everywhere in Burgundy, it is said, the *fermier*, either as owner or as agent, was getting control of the *seigneuries*.[3] The *fermier* might be a small business man, buying the farm of the dues, or exploiting seigniorial mills and so on for a fixed sum, and taking his profit out of whatever over and above this sum he could raise. Or he might be a well-to-do peasant, often also controlling small artisan enterprises and acting as a middleman for the sale of crops, hides, wool, or any other products of the land.[4] Or he might be a *procureur*, notary or other kind of lawyer. In his *Tableau de Paris*, Mercier describes the notaries as much more financiers than lawyers, 'true Proteuses, go-ahead financiers, speculators'. He adds, 'The profession has become so prosperous that from the highest to the lowest every bourgeois wants to put his son in the office of a notary.'[5]

There were widespread complaints of the excesses of the seigniorial agents or collectors. The *feudistes*, or *commissaires à terrier*, especially when they were paid on a

---

[1] Lefebvre, *Études*, p. 65; Bouloiseau, *Cahiers de Rouen*, ii, p. 158; Garaud, *La Révolution et la propriété foncière*, p. 172; Savina et Bernard, *Cahiers de Quimper et de Concarneau*, i, p. xviii.

[2] Doniol, *La Révolution française et la féodalité*, pp. 27–8.

[3] Saint-Jacob, *Les paysans de la Bourgogne*, pp. 428–9.

[4] Méthivier, *L'ancien régime*, p. 24.

[5] Mercier, *Tableau de Paris*, i, p. 143.

commission basis, had an interest in screwing up the seigniorial dues to the highest pitch.[1] They were bitterly attacked in the *cahiers*.[2] By discovering and exploiting rights of escheat, it was said, they were a menace to heirs.[3] D'Aiguillon, in the National Assembly on the night of 4 August, argued that the *seigneurs* allowed, or by exacting excessive payments from their agents even encouraged them, to exploit the system.[4] The *fermiers* were denounced for the rapacity and bad faith which they exhibited as collectors of ordinary rents as well as of seigniorial dues.[5] The *cahiers* of the Autunois say that its farms were worked by peasants who formerly shared the produce or profits equally with the proprietor. Now the collection is let out to *fermiers*, who overcharge the cultivator and leave him only a quarter of the proceeds. Their word is taken for any advances they claim to have made to the peasant during the course of the lease, although, it was alleged, most of the *fermiers* cannot read or keep books.[6]

The author of a treatise on seigniorial rights compares the *fermier* to 'a ravaging wolf let loose on the land, who extracts the last sou out of it, crushes the people with burdens, reduces them to beggary, forces the peasants to desert the land, and renders the master who finds himself compelled to tolerate these exactions odious.'[7] When

[1] Aulard, *La Révolution française et le régime féodal*, pp. 58–9.
[2] *E.g.* Bois, *Paysans de l'Ouest*, p. 197.
[3] J. McManners, *French Ecclesiastical Society under the ancien régime* (1961), p. 116.
[4] *Réimpression de l'ancien moniteur* (1840), I, p. 284.
[5] F. Mège, *Les cahiers des paroisses d'Auvergne en 1789* (1899), p. 112.
[6] Desplaces de Charmasse, *Cahiers d'Autun*, p. 37.
[7] Renauldon, *Traité historique . . . des droits seigneuriaux*, p. 5: cited in Garaud, *La Révolution et la propriété foncière*, p. 73.

in Auvergne one *fermier* was knocked down and nearly killed, and another fired at, the *sous-délégué* excused the inhabitants because of the conduct of the *fermiers*.[1]

The best preserved, and the most universally hated, of the seigniorial rights, were the *banalités* of mill, wine or olive press, and oven. Of these, the right of the banal mill was the most valuable and most widespread.[2] It was the most widely denounced abuse in the *cahiers*.[3] The millers with rights of *banalité* exercised a stranglehold over the bread trade. Bakers complained that if they got their flour elsewhere than at the mill of the *banalité*, they had to pay a fine to the miller,[4] and that at the banal mill they had to pay excessive prices.[5] Another result of the millers' monopoly is implied by the demand that certified royal weights should be placed in each mill.[6] The peasants of a Breton parish complain that they have neither weights nor weighing machines, and that if they demand that their flour shall be weighed, the millers know how to add water to make it up to the proper weight.[7] Another complaint is that the *banalités* are an inexhaustible cause of lawsuits.[8] If no one were restricted to purchasing from the seigniorial mill, says another Breton *cahier* sarcastically, all the millers would become honest men.[9]

---

[1] Mège, *Cahiers d'Auvergne*, p. 112.

[2] Saint-Jacob, *Paysans de la Bourgogne*, pp. 421–2.

[3] References to justify this statement are too many to be given.

[4] R. Jouanne, *Cahiers des doléances des corps et corporations de la ville d'Alençon* (1929), p. xix.

[5] Savina et Bernard, *Cahiers de Quimper et de Concarneau*, I, p. 26.

[6] Desplaces de Charmasse, *Cahiers d'Autun*, pp. 155, 278–9 and elsewhere.

[7] Savina et Bernard, *Cahiers de Quimper et de Concarneau*, I, p. 26.

[8] Jouanne, *Cahiers d'Alençon*, p. 52.

[9] Savina et Bernard, *Cahiers de Quimper et de Concarneau*, I, p. 26.

The blame for the abuse of banal rights was not confined to the millers, as the story of one *seigneur* reveals. He abandoned his seigniorial oven in 1770 and the villagers had to build their own ovens, which they did. In 1775 the *seigneur's* steward announced that he intended to restore the seigniorial oven, and that any inhabitant who made use of his own oven, instead of the lord's, would have to pay a fine annually.[1] It was sometimes added in the complaints against the millers that they were forced to rely on fraud because of the excessive rents that were exacted by the *seigneurs* or their agents.[2]

The *banalités*, then, were a patent and flagrant abuse, and one which was generally condemned. Yet even here the attitude of the town *cahiers* is hesitant. The *cahier* of Mirecourt, while it asked for their abolition, stipulated that the same millers should continue to have the monopoly of the mills.[3] A miller in the Meuse, after the legislation of 4–11 August had ended the system of *banalités*, demanded compensation, on the ground that he had purchased the right in good faith.[4] If the *banalités* represented feudalism, the *cahiers* of the towns showed little anxiety to be rid of it. But can they be regarded in any real sense as feudal, whatever may have been their origin in remoter centuries? They seem to me to be much better described, in more modern terms, as a commercial racket.

[1] C. Étienne, *Cahiers de doléances des bailliages des généralités de Metz et de Nancy* (1912), ii, p. 149.
[2] C. Anglade, 'Un exemple de la réaction nobiliaire', *Annales du Midi* (1953), pp. 175–6; Savina et Bernard, *Cahiers de Quimper et de Concarneau*, i, p. 26.
[3] Martin, *Cahiers de Mirecourt*, p. 7.
[4] Sagnac et Caron, *Les Comités des droits féodaux*, pp. 207–8.

The whole matter of seigniorial dues takes on a different aspect when we look at what actually happened, instead of seeking for illustrations to support a preconceived theory. There is ample evidence that the peasantry was very conscious of the burden they represented in the years before the French Revolution, and it is probable that the burden was increasing. This is what is commonly called the 'feudal reaction'. It would be premature to suggest that we know in sufficient detail the situation in different parts of France to be sure of any one particular interpretation; but perhaps we already know enough to feel safe in suggesting that the term 'feudal reaction' is a misnomer. Even if the surviving or revived seigniorial rights could be described as feudal, what was taking place was certainly not a reaction to the past. If they were becoming a heavier burden it was, as can be most plainly seen in the case of the *banalités*, because of their increasing commercialisation. They had entered the nexus of buying and selling, and those who bought, and also of course many of those who did not sell, were determined to get their money's worth. There is at least some excuse for believing that the revolution in the French countryside was not against feudalism but against a growing commercialisation; and that it was not a 'bourgeois' movement but on the contrary was directed partly against the penetration of urban financial interests into the countryside.

There remains one final line of retreat for those who wish to identify the peasant movement against seigniorial dues with a 'bourgeois revolt against feudalism'. This consists in the discovery of a class called, among many other names, the 'rural bourgeoisie', which is supposed to have led and profited by the movement against the seigniorial system. If it did so, this was clearly in opposition to the urban bourgeoisie, which makes the assumption of a single bourgeois class interest difficult to maintain. Something more will have to be said of this supposed rural bourgeoisie in a later chapter, when the manifold inconsistencies in the conception, which make it untenable, will have to be pointed out.[1]

There is really no alternative to accepting what every historian who had looked at the evidence would have been bound to have accepted if it had not been for intellectual enslavement to a theory. The abolition of seigniorial dues was the work of the peasantry, unwillingly accepted by the men who drew up the town and *bailliage cahiers*, and forced on the National Assembly through the fear inspired by a peasant revolt. It follows that the 'overthrow of feudalism by the bourgeoisie' takes on very much the appearance of the myth I suggested it was in a lecture some eight years ago. So far, however, the discussion has turned mainly on the nature of the so-called feudalism of the eighteenth century. Even if it is agreed that by feudalism can only be meant the survival of a system of seigniorial dues, and that these were abolished as a result of the action of the peasantry, and against the wishes and interests of the urban elements who led the revolution, this is not to deny that in other respects there may have been a 'bourgeois' revolution. We have therefore to ask who, in fact, were the revolutionary bourgeois.

[1] *V. infra*, pp. 107–9.

CHAPTER VI

WHO WERE THE REVOLUTIONARY BOURGEOIS?

Historians are generally agreed that the revolution was a bourgeois revolution. 'The class', writes Mathiez, 'which was going to take control of the Revolution was fully conscious of its strength and its rights.'[1] M. Albert Soboul echoes the same judgement: 'The commercial and industrial bourgeoisie had a penetrating consciousness of social evolution and of the economic power which it represented. It guided, with a sure awareness of its interests, the revolution to its objective.'[2] All this is so clear and obvious and simple that it tempts one to ask some simple and obvious questions. In the first place, was it a class? Mathiez, I think, would have had no doubts. M. Soboul represents a later generation of historians and cannot escape the influence of a more sophisticated analysis. In contradiction to his earlier verdict, he says, 'The bourgeoisie was diverse, it did not form a homogeneous class.'[3]

A detailed analysis is provided by Georges Lefebvre, who divides the eighteenth-century French bourgeoisie into five groups—(a) the bourgeois proper 'living nobly and on his property', (b) members of the royal administra-

[1] Mathiez, *La Révolution française*, I, p. 48.
[2] Soboul, *Précis*, p. 38.
[3] *Ibid.*, p. 58.

tion, *officiers*, proprietors of venal offices, some of them ennobled, (c) lawyers—notaries, *procureurs*, *avocats*, (d) members of the liberal professions—doctors, scientists, writers, artists, (e) the world of finance and commerce— shipbuilders, wholesale traders, entrepreneurs, and the upper grades of financiers starting with the Farmers General.[1] Within each of these groups there were widely divergent levels of wealth and status. Their attitude to the revolution varied greatly, as did the effect of the revolution on them, though the use of the general term bourgeoisie has concealed these differences. Since French historians themselves invariably use it, I may have to do so in referring to their views, but this must not be taken as implying any acceptance of the existence of a large, uniform, bourgeois class.

There is a general assumption that the eighteenth century witnessed the rise of the middle classes in France as a whole. I have mentioned above the ambiguities involved in the idea of the rise of classes.[2] Leaving this on one side, we may at least ask whether the general assumption is true of all the different elements mentioned above. There is ample evidence for the increasing prosperity in the eighteenth century of the world of finance and business. Finance, above all, was the way of rising in the world: the possession of wealth—in sufficient quantity—was a key that opened nearly every door. References to *hommes nouveaux*, *nouveaux riches*, *conquérants financiers*, abound in the literature of the eighteenth century. Marion refers to 'the ostentation of a "new man" who has become the

---

[1] G. Lefebvre, *La Révolution française* (1951), pp. 48–50.
[2] *V. supra*, p. 22.

master of great estates by financial dealings'.[1] Sénac de Meilhan, writing at the time, draws attention to the way in which diverse social groups were coming together. 'The children of financiers', he writes, 'were raised to positions in the magistrature, and reached the highest places, even in the government. The wealth of the financiers became the recourse of great families in difficulties, and marriage connections multiplied between the greatest noble houses and rich financiers.'[2] 'Persons of standing', wrote Duclos in 1750, perhaps with some exaggeration, 'have already lost the right of despising finance, since there are few who are not connected with it by marriage.'[3]

Secondly, there were the greater merchants, obviously rising in wealth and influence in ports like Bordeaux and Nantes, and also, though less spectacularly, in a more industrial city like Rouen.[4] These formed only a small group, a fact which has been obscured by the use of the term merchant, as has been said above,[5] to include a range extending from the merchant princes of Bordeaux down to the village pedlar. Far from there being any sense of solidarity amongst such 'merchants', there was intense enmity: the wealthy *négociants* had only contempt for their lesser fellows.

A regular jungle of terms is included in the idea of the merchant—*négociant, trafiquand, grossier, commerçant, ré-*

[1] M. Marion, *Histoire financière de la France*, I, p. 196.

[2] Sénac de Meilhan, *Du gouvernement, des mœurs, des conditions en France avant la Révolution* (1795), p. 69.

[3] C.-P. Duclos, *Considérations sur les mœurs de ce siècle*, ed. F. C. Green (1939), p. 125.

[4] Bouloiseau, *Cahier de Rouen*, I, p. lxiii.

[5] *V. supra*, p. 19.

gratteur, détailleur—and we can never take any of them at its face value, because it was only human nature for a merchant to describe himself by a term which strictly applied to a higher grade. To refer again to an illustration mentioned earlier, the Breton secret agent, who served the English from Jersey, Noël Prigent, said of himself that he was '*né négociant*'. When, on one of his missions to the royalists in the Vendée, armed with a letter of credit from the British government as its 'ambassador', he was captured, the revolutionary authorities made great fun of the pretensions of 'this Prigent', whom, they said, they had known when he was pushing a barrow round the streets of St Malo selling apples and pears.[1] Even if they exaggerated, this particular *négociant* at least could be described, not implausibly, as a barrow-boy.

Even in the Constituent Assembly there were many described as merchants who came from towns far too small for it to be supposed that they could support a substantial commerce. The intendant of Alençon wrote that trade in his province was '*fort peu de chose*' and that its merchants were '*fort peu aisés*'.[2] This does not mean that they were doomed to remain so. A recent study of the area that was to be the department of the Sarthe suggests that the small business men of the little bourgs were profiting by their close connection with the peasants to act as middlemen, selling to and buying from them, exploiting their artisan labour, operating as seigniorial agents, buying small patches of land, gaining by the rise in land

---

[1] Cobban, 'The Beginnings of the Channel Isles Correspondence', *English Historical Review*, LXXVII (1962), p. 47 and n. 5.

[2] Jouanne, *Cahiers d'Alençon*, p. xv.

rents, building up their property both before and during the revolution.[1] In spite of the great range of wealth or comparative poverty that was represented in it, at both ends of the scale the trading interest seems on the whole to have been rising—but rising into what?

In this connection little need be said of the industrialists. They were few and uninfluential, and they played little part in the history of the revolution. As St Simon wrote, 'It was not the industrialists who made the revolution. It was the bourgeois'—a verdict which incidentally suggests that industrialists were not normally included in the term 'bourgeois'.

So far, however, I have not mentioned those who in the eighteenth century were the bourgeois proper. These were the *rentiers* and proprietors, living 'nobly', that is, without any occupation, mainly on the income or *rentes* from property, and from government or private loans. By their wealth and manner of life they belonged with the moderately prosperous noblesse, and very largely shared its fate—whatever that was—in the revolution. Whether they were rising or not, they were part of the conservative and not the revolutionary section of society.

There remain from Lefebvre's list the *officiers*, holders of venal posts, lesser officials of the royal administration, lawyers and members of the liberal professions. Among these, the description of lawyer is too general to be of use in a social analysis, or it is about as much use as a classification by the possession of a university degree would be to-day. Even among those who filled one or another of the various legal functions, the differences were so great as to

[1] Bois, *Paysans de l'Ouest*, p. 367.

make any common treatment misleading. Of the largest, clearly identifiable, single group, however, we can make some positive statements. A section of society which was definitely not rising in wealth, and was barely holding its own in social status, was that of the *officiers*. The test of this is the decline in the value of venal offices and the failure to find purchasers for them.[1] The decline seems to have been general, from the *parlements* downwards,[2] though until the end of the eighteenth century it was much less marked in the offices of the *parlements* than in those of the *présidiaux, élections, maréchaussées* and other local courts.[3] One specific example, from the lowest end of the scale, is provided by the *huissiers* and sergeants at Rouen, who complained in 1789 that their offices, worth 3,000 livres each in 1700, were now only worth 300, and that out of 22, 12 were vacant.[4] Similarly, the *bailliage* of Rouen, which had formerly had 29 *officiers*, in 1788 only had 16.[5]

As the commercial and financial classes were rising, so, it seems, the class of venal officers was declining. The inevitable result was a conflict between the rising and declining groups, which particularly took the form of a struggle for control of the towns. While the *bailliage* offices remained in the hereditary possession of the old

[1] *Cf.* Ford, *Robe and Sword*, p. 149.

[2] *E.g.* in Dauphiné a *charge* of president in the *parlement* of Grenoble, which had been worth 110,000 livres in 1665, had fallen by 1764 to 60,000 livres; while the office of *conseiller*, formerly worth 66,000 livres, by 1780 was a mere 19,000. J. Egret, *Le parlement de Dauphiné, et les affaires publiques dans la deuxième moitié du XVIIIe siècle* (1942), I, p. 18; II, p. 36.

[3] Ford, *loc. cit.*

[4] Bouloiseau, *Cahiers de Rouen*, I, pp. 54–5.

[5] *Ibid.*, pp. 21–2.

royal officers, places in the municipal government were bought up by members of the wealthier commercial class. In Rouen, dominated by the greater traders,[1] these controlled the municipality and the consular jurisdiction.[2] The *officiers*, in *chambre des comptes*, *bureau des finances*, sovereign courts and so on, constituted a conservative faction which opposed the reforms supported by the merchants and some of the lawyers.[3] A similar conflict developed in Bordeaux, where, in the elections to the États Généraux in 1789, the lawyers, with public support, overthrew the previously predominant influence of the great merchants.[4] Vire, on the other hand, had been dominated by the *officiers*.[5]

The municipal struggle also took the form of rivalry over the administration of justice, the *bailliage* judges having to face the competition not only of the intendants and their subordinates, but also of the consular jurisdiction of the towns. In an effort to protect the interests of the royal courts, a decree of 7 April 1759, confirmed in January 1764, restricted consular jurisdiction to the limits of the *bailliage* or *sénéchaussée*.[6]

This was only part of a general struggle for precedence and influence in the towns, waged between the business world and the liberal professions.[7] To a certain extent it

[1] *Ibid.*, I, p. 221.

[2] *Ibid.*, I, p. xiii.

[3] *Ibid.*, I, p. lxiv.

[4] M. Lhéritier, *La Fin de l'ancien régime et la préparation des États généraux (1787–1789). La Révolution à Bordeaux* (1942), p. 232.

[5] P. Nicolle, *Histoire de Vire pendant la Révolution (1789–1800)* (1923), p. 36.

[6] P. de Saint-Jacob, 'Histoire économique et sociale dans les archives de la jurisdiction consulaire de Dijon (1715–1789)', *Bulletin de la société d'histoire moderne*, no. 1 (1958), p. 6.

[7] Reinhard, 'Sur l'histoire de la Révolution française', p. 560.

may be justifiable to describe it as a struggle between a rising and a falling bourgeoisie. In the view of M. Labrousse the former was the dominant element. The eighteenth century, he argues, was a great period of economic expansion, of growth in bourgeois wealth and power, which led up to a 'revolution of prosperity'.[1] This is on the unproved, and indeed mistaken, assumption that the prosperous merchants, financiers and manufacturers inspired and led the revolution. The reverse is patently true. That the *officiers* and the men of the liberal professions prepared and directed the revolution, and that the business men were not its prime movers, was the sounder view of Lefebvre.[2] Professor Marcel Reinhard agrees that the men of business played no leading part in the revolution.[3] An analysis of the membership of the revolutionary assemblies, showing the overwhelming preponderance of *bailliage* officers and members of the liberal professions, helps to confirm the same view.[4] This was the revolutionary bourgeoisie.

But if Lefebvre's scrupulous regard for historical evidence forced him to recognise that the leadership of the revolution was not in the hands of the rising commercial, financial and industrial class, he argued that all the same it represented their interests. The revolution, writes Lefebvre, 'for the first time in Europe proclaimed liberty of enterprise', it opened the way to capitalism.[5] Professor Labrousse similarly sees the social philosophy of the

[1] C.-E. Labrousse, *La crise de l'économie française à la fin de l'ancien régime et au début de la Révolution* (1944), p. xlviii.

[2] Lefebvre, *La Révolution française* (1951), p. 75.

[3] Reinhard, *op. cit.*, p. 561.

[4] Cobban, *The Myth of the French Revolution* (1955), pp. 23-5.

[5] Lefebvre, 'Le mythe de la Révolution française', p. 343.

revolution in the abolition of corporations and trading companies, in free trade and enclosures.[1] This is the bourgeois, capitalist policy that is said to have triumphed in the revolution, and it will repay a little closer examination if we are to understand the composition and ideas of the revolutionary bourgeoisie.

Undoubtedly the corporations, trading companies, *maîtrises* and *jurandes*, which exercised a stranglehold on French trade and industry, were breaking down in the second half of the eighteenth century. The *métier libre* was already widespread and work in *jurandes* the exception.[2] Efforts were made to encourage the people of the countryside to take up the manufactures which were restricted in towns by *jurandes*. An *arrêt* of 7 November 1762 authorised inhabitants of the country to buy raw materials and tools for the manufacture of all kinds of fabric.[3] For a short period, when Turgot was Controller-General, the *maîtrises* and *jurandes* had been abolished, only for the decree to be reversed on his fall. The corporations were upheld by the *parlements* as a means of controlling the workers, 'those beings born to trouble society' as the Parlement of Paris put it in 1776,[4] but by 1789, though in their *cahiers* the corporations naturally opposed their own abolition, many more *cahiers* were in favour of it.[5] The legislation of the revolution completed the process of their elimination.

[1] R. Mousnier et E. Labrousse, *Le XVIIIe siècle* (1953), p. 391 *seqq.*

[2] R. Picard, *Les cahiers de 1789 et les classes ouvrières* (1910), p. 68.

[3] A. Colomès, *Les ouvriers de textile dans le Champagne troyenne, 1730–1752* (1943), p. 31.

[4] Picard, *op. cit.*, p. 70; J. Flammermont, *Remontrances du parlement de Paris au XVIIIe siècle* (1895–97), III, p. 310.

[5] Picard, *op. cit.*, p. 86.

There were other respects in which revolutionary legislation on economic matters continued *ancien régime* trends. The *loi le Chapelier*, banning combinations of workers to raise wages, has been described as a new, revolutionary measure of defence by the bourgeois against the workers. This, said Braesch, is to judge it by modern ideas.[1] Henri Sée pointed out that it merely repeated the legislation of the *ancien régime*.[2] Advanced economic thought before the revolution, as represented by Turgot, had developed something like a theory of the iron law of wages as a justification for keeping these down to the minimum necessary for existence.[3] Necker, on the contrary, held that the workers were exploited, that technical progress had been of no advantage to them, and argued for government intervention.[4] Such a view found practically no support in the revolutionary assemblies. A petition from the workers of Beauvais led the *rapporteur* of the National Assembly to write, on 4 October 1790, warning the municipal officers that 'the wages of workers are not within their competence, these can only be fixed by natural laws'.[5] For any different views we will have to look below the level of the revolutionary assemblies.[6]

An attempt has been made to discriminate between different sections of the revolutionary leadership in this

[1] F. Braesch, *1789: l'année cruciale* (1941), p. 251.
[2] H. Sée, *L'évolution commerciale et industrielle de la France sous l'ancien régime* (1925), p. 355.
[3] H. Grange, 'Turgot et Necker devant le problème des salaires', *Annales historiques de la Révolution française*, no. 146 (1957), p. 21.
[4] *Ibid.*, pp. 25–6, 28, 30.
[5] F. Gerbaux et Ch. Schmidt, *Procès-verbaux des comités d'agriculture et de commerce* (1906), I, p. 565.
[6] *Cf. infra*, pp. 157–8.

respect, and to attribute such 'bourgeois' views specifically to one section of it, distinguishable by its social composition and political affiliations. This is the so-called 'bourgeoisie girondine, bourgeoisie d'affaires'.[1] The chief evidence given for the belief that there was a socially distinct 'Girondin' party is the identification of certain leaders of this supposed party, such as Isnard, Kervélégan, Buzot, Pétion, as men of substance. The whole legend of the Girondin bourgeoisie is a model example of what results from ignoring the most elementary techniques of social science. In the first place, before the existence of a large, coherent and influential social grouping can be postulated, a rather bigger sample than some half a dozen specially selected cases is needed. Secondly, even if we could identify a substantial Girondin party at the centre, and make a social analysis of its composition, no satisfactory conclusions could be drawn without knowing how this compared with the composition of the whole group of which it formed part, that is, of the Legislative Assembly and Convention as a whole. As for the 'Girondins' of the provinces, hardly any attempt has been made even to identify them.

In his study of the Girondins, Dr Sydenham has shown that the existence of a large and coherent Girondin party in the Convention, consisting of some 200 members, backed by a great body of opinion in the country, is a myth, created for propaganda purposes by the Mountain.[2] The reality was the existence of a few loosely connected

[1] A. Soboul, 'Sur la fortune des Girondins', *Annales historiques de la Révolution française*, no. 136 (1954), pp. 257–60.

[2] M. J. Sydenham, *The Girondins* (1961).

political groups, the Brissotins, Rolandists, Pétainists, as they were sometimes called, and including leading members of the deputation of the Gironde. In all, some twenty or twenty-five loosely associated deputies can be identified. They exhibited little in the way of a common policy and no political coherence, and were in any case too few to be statistically significant. Further, the belief that this supposed Girondin party represented the wealthier middle class, as contrasted with their poorer Jacobin opponents in the Convention, is a pure supposition with little factual basis. M. Soboul indeed writes of '*la bourgeoisie montagnarde, haute bourgeoisie souvent*' and agrees that doubtless most of the Mountain was equally of bourgeois origin.[1] Yet he still believes that the struggle between the Mountain and their opponents in the Convention, who were later labelled Girondins, took on the form of a class conflict.[2]

The failure of the attempt to distinguish the social composition of the 'Girondin' group from that of the huge majority of the Convention has led some historians to fall back on a supposed difference in their economic and social principles or policies. Unfortunately, it is hardly in dispute that practically the whole Convention, with at most only a handful of exceptions, was devoted to the new economic orthodoxy of *laissez faire* and individualism. The argument, however, is that while one party, the Girondin, clung to its bourgeois principles at all costs, the Mountain, in the interests of national defence, willingly adopted (or alternatively, had forced on it,

[1] Soboul, *Précis*, pp. 228–9.
[2] *Ibid.*

because both views are expressed) a policy which for a time protected the economic interests of the masses.[1] Even if this view of the economic policy of the Mountain is correct, it should not affect our general verdict on the social policy of the revolutionaries, in which the economic measures of the Mountain have to be seen as a temporary aberration.

What, then, was this social and economic policy? The accepted view cannot be better given than in the words of M. Soboul. 'Thus', he writes, 'was the traditional economic order overthrown. Doubtless the bourgeoisie was before 1789 the master of production and exchange. But *laisser faire, laisser passer* freed its commercial and industrial activities from the fetters of privilege and monopoly. Capitalist production had been born and had begun to develop in the framework of a still feudal property system: the framework was now broken. The bourgeoisie of the Constituent Assembly accelerated the evolution by liberating the economy.'[2]

This seems an extremely plausible theory: difficulties only begin to arise when we look at the facts. In the first place, of course, we need not confine the judgement to the Constituent Assembly; nor—apart from the interlude represented by the rule of the Committee of Public Safety—do I think that M. Soboul intends to do so. Whether the organisation of industry in France was capitalist before the revolution has been a subject of some debate. Jaurès, Levasseur, Germain Martin, des Cilleuls, Picard, Ardachev, said that it was; Kovalesky, Tarlé,

[1] *Ibid.*
[2] *Ibid.*, p. 159.

Petrov, Loutchitsky argued that France remained a *pays agricole*.[1] This is mainly a matter of terminology. The essential point is to decide if the revolution does in fact represent an important stage in the economic history of France, and whether the direction in which its influence operated was in fact that which is suggested.

The questions that need to be asked can be put in specific terms. Did the revolution promote a policy of freedom of trade and industry? Did it liberate, or in any way change, the role of finance? What was its influence on the commerce and the industry of France? These should not be regarded as superfluous questions, and in seeking for answers the fact that the revolutionary bourgeoisie was primarily the declining class of *officiers* and the lawyers and other professional men, and not the businessmen of commerce and industry, should warn us against any preconceived conclusions.

[1] A. Choulguine (K. A. Shul'gin), 'L'organisation capitaliste de l'industrie existait-elle en France à la veille de la Révolution?', *Revue d'histoire économique et sociale*, x (1922), pp. 184–218.

CHAPTER VII

ECONOMIC CONSEQUENCES OF THE REVOLUTION

THE abolition of privileged corporations in industry was one of the earliest effects of the revolution. Journeymen who imagined that the object was to let them set up in business on their own soon learnt that they were mistaken.[1] Who in fact gained, and who lost, by this final abolition of obsolete and anachronistic institutions, which had only survived (or been revived) because they served the direct financial interests of the crown, and what effect did it have on French trade and industry? These are questions which would be worth investigation. Presumably they have not been investigated so far because it has been assumed that we know the answer: that the result was the liberation of French economy from feudal bonds and its simultaneous subjection to capitalism. This book will have been written to no purpose if it does not suggest that the repetition of such meaningless clichés is no substitute for historical research.

A second economic consequence of the revolution, also frequently commented on, was the freeing of trade in the interests, it is said, of bourgeois economic individualism. Again, it is desirable to ask just what was the free trade

[1] *V. infra*, p. 158.

that the revolutionaries wanted, and here enough work has been done for us to attempt an answer. In the first place, it presumably meant the abolition of trading monopolies, chiefly in colonial trade. Oddly enough, by a decree of 8 March 1790, the Constituent Assembly declared that it had no intention of innovating in any branches of commerce with the colonies:[1] this was equivalent to deciding to continue the system of restriction; and the decree was passed in response to addresses and petitions from the commercial cities. These petitions may have been got up by the West Indian interest; but they represent the influence of one sector of the commercial interest and it was exercised against and not in favour of freedom of trade.[2]

Another practical issue was that posed by the Treaty of Commerce with England. Arthur Young said that in Bordeaux, whose wine trade stood to profit by the treaty, it was popular.[3] Elsewhere, however, he had to report bitter hostility.[4] By a decree of 1 March 1793 the Treaty of Commerce was denounced,[5] but well before this the pressure for a more restrictive commercial policy had reached a high pitch.

There was a good deal of variation in the views expressed on freedom of trade in 1789, obviously depending on the ways in which different groups thought it would affect their own interests. Thus, the larger employers and

[1] *L'Ancien moniteur*, III, p. 553.

[2] M. Lhéritier, *Liberté (1789–1790). Les Girondins: Bordeaux et la Révolution française* (1947), pp. 138–9.

[3] Arthur Young, *Travels in France*, 25 August 1787.

[4] *E.g.* at Abbeville, 19 May 1787.

[5] F. L. Nussbaum, *Commercial policy in the French Revolution. A study of the career of G. J. A. Ducher* (1923), p. 77.

the workers in the textile industry of Reims called for absolute liberty of trade, whereas the commercial interests were opposed to it.[1] In Rouen, on the other hand, it was the bigger merchants who demanded the abolition of regulations on manufacture and the freeing of commerce from restrictions.[2]

It would be superfluous to attempt to collect the many other examples of local variations to be found. What has been said already should show that we cannot take it for granted that we know what the men of 1789 meant by free trade. Very few, indeed, meant freedom of trade between nations. The *cahiers* of Rouen that called for freedom of trade were only directed against the municipal taxes on articles of consumption—the *octrois* and *aides*.[3] In the main, however, the demand for freedom of trade must be understood in relation to the century-old movement for the abolition of the internal customs, and it is shown by Dr John Bosher that this movement was led throughout, and ultimately brought to success, not by the representatives of commercial and industrial interests, but by reforming officials.[4]

Merchants and manufacturers sometimes supported the movement, but commercial interests in such provinces as Lorraine, Trois Évêchés, Alsace, Guyenne and Brittany, feared the effects of the abolition of internal customs on their own trade and manufacture. Manufacturing interests tended on the whole to support, and commercial

---

[1] G. Laurent, *Reims et la région rémoise*, pp. 135–6.
[2] Bouloiseau, *Cahiers de Rouen*, I, pp. cxvi–cxvii.
[3] *Ibid.*, I, p. cxviii.
[4] In his forthcoming book on the struggle for the abolition of the internal customs in eighteenth-century France.

interests to oppose, the reform.[1] By 1789 there was a fairly wide support for the abolition of internal customs; but, concentrated exclusively on their immediate concerns, what business interests wanted was a larger domestic market, along with protection against foreign competition. Their petitions were not for general reform, but for freedom from specific internal dues.[2] Similarly, the merchants of the towns wanted freedom for their own trade and prohibitions on that of any possible rivals. Against the travelling merchants or pedlars of the countryside there was a widespread outcry by the *tiers état* of the towns.[3]

As for international commerce, the revolution speedily brought an end to such ideas of freer trade as the last years of the *ancien régime* had evolved. In August 1790 the Deputies Extraordinary of Commerce[4] urged the Committee of Agriculture and Commerce to take into consideration a project for a Navigation Act.[5] The supposed Girondin leaders, especially Brissot and Clavière, who should, if as is alleged they were the special representatives of the wealthy commercial interests, have supported this agitation, on the contrary were predisposed against restrictive commercial legislation.[6] The leader of the movement for a Navigation policy, the Alsatian G. J. A.

---

[1] *Ibid.*

[2] *Ibid.*

[3] *Cf.* Grille, *Introduction aux Mémoires*, II, pp. 104–6; Loriquet, *Cahiers du Pas-de-Calais*, I, pp. 33, 52, 75, 82, 100, 157.

[4] The Deputies of Commerce had come to be agents rather of the Crown than of the towns they were supposed to represent. Extraordinary deputies were therefore called to Paris in 1788 from the mercantile cities. Bosher, *loc. cit.*

[5] Nussbaum, *op. cit.*, p. 44.

[6] *Ibid.*, p. 84.

Ducher, said bitterly of them, in April 1794, 'The same men who desired to declare war on all Europe, to extend the habit of speculation to the smallest villages of France [was this a reference to their opposition to control of the corn trade?], were also those who obstructed the Navigation Act and tried to overthrow the customs barrier which protected national commerce.'[1] On the other hand a report by Barère of 21 September 1793 called for a Navigation Act,[2] which was passed on 18 October, after the Mountain had come into power.[3] Holland Rose argued in general terms that Napoleon's Continental System was inherited from the revolutionaries;[4] and this view has been substantiated with a much fuller and more satisfactory documentation by Nussbaum.[5] But what Napoleon inherited was the policy of the Mountain not of the supposititious Gironde. It would be more logical to say, then, that the Mountain was the true representative of commercial interests. I do not suggest this, because I believe that the whole line of argument is based on a misinterpretation of the social composition and interests of the revolutionary assemblies.

So far this discussion has been confined to the ideas and policies of the revolutionaries. It is not difficult to agree that the businessmen of France were anxious to promote such legislation as they thought would be to their own interests. During the revolution, freed from the opposi-

---

[1] *Ibid.*, p. 193.

[2] *Ibid.*, pp. 107–8.

[3] *Ibid.*, p. 113.

[4] 'Napoleon and English Commerce', *English Historical Review*, VIII (1893), p. 704.

[5] Nussbaum, *op. cit.*, p. 291 *seqq.*

tion of small privileged groups, they were able to secure their emancipation from a network of *ancien régime* monopolies, privileges and barriers. But is this the great bourgeois, or capitalist, revolution that we have been told of? Did it change, in kind or degree, the basic economic structure of France? Did it establish a new class of great capitalist entrepreneurs in control of the government and the destinies of France? These are the meaningful questions to be asked, and they have to be answered in terms of actual economic facts.

The economic consequences of the revolution, like those of any other historical event, were not, of course, necessarily those that were aimed at. Political, or other, interests may conflict with economic ones, and the latter do not always emerge victorious from the conflict. One determining factor which influenced, and perhaps even dominated the economic situation, was a result of the revolutionary war. This was the loss of France's external markets and, as a result, the collapse of foreign trade.[1] Napoleon's attempt to compensate for the loss of extra-European supplies and outlets by the creation of a grandiose continental economic empire was largely a failure —not least because protectionist policies, inherited from the revolution and the *ancien régime*, led to an attempt to exploit the rest of Europe in the interests of France.

The collapse of the trade of Bordeaux and the other great Atlantic ports came early in the revolution. The prosperity of Marseille could not survive English naval

[1] F. Crouzet, 'Les conséquences économiques de la Révolution à propos d'un inédit de Sir Francis d'Invernois', *Annales historiques de la Révolution française*, no. 168 (1962), pp. 214–15.

successes in the Mediterranean. Under Napoleon the only trade which flourished was the smuggling trade, which seeped in and made its way across Europe through all the cracks and crannies in the rambling frontiers of the ramshackle Napoleonic Empire. Not until after 1825 did French external trade return to the level it had reached in 1788.[1]

It has hardly been claimed by any historian that the revolution was other than a disaster for France's colonial and foreign trade. There has been an attempt to assume, however, that it did at least promote a large scale industrialisation. Professor François Crouzet has recently given us some useful corrective facts on this subject. Even in comparison with 1789, a year of industrial depression, there was, he says, a decline in the woollen industry in France.[2] The linen trade suffered terribly during the revolution,[3] and in many parts, especially the West, never returned to its former prosperity.[4] Cotton, which has been described as the only industry able to stand up to '*le mauvais temps économique de la Révolution*',[5] may have been helped in this by the introduction of machines;[6] but it has been shown that most of the larger spinning mills set up before 1789 experienced grave difficulties during the revolution.[7] At Lyon the silk and other

---

[1] H. Sée, *L'Évolution commerciale et industrielle de la France sous l'ancien régime* (1925), p. 247.

[2] Crouzet, *op. cit.*, pp. 199, 202.

[3] *Ibid.*, p. 202.

[4] *Ibid.*, pp. 202, 204.

[5] *Ibid.*, p. 205, citing A. Chabert, *Essai sur les mouvements des revenus et de l'activité économique en France de 1798 à 1820* (1949), p. 130.

[6] But this was bitterly opposed. *V. infra*, pp. 158-9.

[7] Crouzet, *op. cit.*, p. 205, citing Ch. Ballot, *L'introduction du machinisme dans l'industrie française* (1923), pp. 67, 73-5, 80, 82.

industries declined.[1] The view that the growth of the commercial capitalism of Lyon was a result of, or at least was posterior to, the revolution does not survive an examination of its major industry, the silk trade. In so far as the revolution overthrew the *ancien régime* cadres of Lyonnais trade and industry, the Empire restored them.[2] A study of the merchants of Toulouse finds them also under the Empire very much what they had been in 1789. 'The most ambitious attained the positions they had envied, others enriched themselves by the acquisition of *biens nationaux*. The Empire found most of the merchants again in a position almost identical with that which they had occupied in 1789.' For them the revolution had been a mere '*brassage en surface*'.[3] Altogether, subsequent research has continued to confirm the verdict of Henri Sée that the revolutionary period held up French industrial development.[4]

The role of the financiers during the revolution can be dealt with quite briefly. They had established their living space in France at least as early as the wars of Louis XIV. The great financiers of the *ancien régime*, who have been referred to above,[5] were by no means the least privileged section of French society. Their unpopularity was the measure of their wealth and influence. The revolution was certainly not their revolution. Some, like many of the great Farmers General, paid for their former glory

[1] Crouzet, *op. cit.*, p. 207.

[2] J. Labasse, *La commerce des soies à Lyon sous Napoléon et la crise de 1811* (1957), p. 127.

[3] G. Marinière, 'Les marchands d'étoffes de Toulouse à la fin du XVIIIe siècle', *Annales du Midi*, t. 70 (1958), p. 308.

[4] Sée, *L'Évolution commerciale et industrielle*, p. 304.

[5] *V. supra*, pp. 55–6.

with their lives, some—especially through the effects of inflation—with their fortunes.

But the possibility of building great financial fortunes remained, and a somewhat lower class of speculators existed to take advantage of it. Though the Committee of Public Safety treated the speculators as public enemies, and suppressed the institutions, like the bourse, through which they operated, only a policy of economic controls, such as none but a small and insignificant minority envisaged,[1] could have changed this. Left-wing pamphleteers give the impression that inflation had made the revolution a happy hunting-ground for speculators, hoarders, monopolists, war contractors, and perhaps they were not mistaken in this. The connection between politics and financial speculation remained an intimate one. To take the place of the established financiers of the *ancien régime*, with their connections with nobles on the make and royal ministers, new men arose, turning to profit their association with revolutionary politicians or Napoleonic officials. Many of the former lost their gains, and some their lives, when the speculative boom of the 'eighties came to an end; but the possibilities of profitable speculation survived.

The financiers were the least politically committed of any section of society. All policies and every government brought grist to their mill. The great Swiss financier, Perregaux, could at the same time be financing the purchases of arms by the Committee of Public Safety, and acting as banker for the royalist agents in France. Out of the Napoleonic Wars an Ouvrard rose to greatness, just

[1] The *enragés*, brought into the light of history by Mathiez.

as a Pâris-Duverney had a century earlier out of the wars of Louis XIV. Finance, in fact, traversed the revolution little changed except in personnel; and one of the permanent conditions of the making of fortunes by speculation is that they can always be lost in the same way. The rise of the new rich is a phenomenon, particularly in revolutionary periods, almost as common as the rise of the middle classes; but unlike the latter it implied no social change but only a change in persons.

The speculative mania which preceded and accompanied the revolution is grossly misinterpreted if it is taken, as it often has been, to signify the rise of a new capitalist order of society. True, the *agioteurs* were, as Professor George V. Taylor has pointed out in a valuable article, essentially different from the merchant capitalists of the old régime 'with its modest partnerships and family enterprises, small-capital putting-out industries, and settled moves and taboos'. But this does not mean that they belonged with, or anticipated, the industrial capitalism of the future. 'The boom of the 1780's, in other words,' Professor Taylor concludes, 'was built on the aristocratic and monarchic institutions of the old order rather than the urban industrial and financial system of the nineteenth century. It exemplified not the so-called Industrial Revolution but the court capitalism of early modern Europe.'[1]

Looking at the economic consequences of the revolution as a whole, they seem astonishingly small for such a great social and political upheaval. This is what M.

---

[1] George V. Taylor, 'The Paris bourse on the eve of the Revolution, 1781–1789', *American Historical Review*, LXVII (1962), pp. 976–7.

Soboul, in spite of his acceptance of the theory of the bourgeois revolution, very frankly recognises. Industrial production under the Directory, he says, was below that of 1789 in cotton. The woollen and metallurgy industries were stagnating. Capitalist concentration remained essentially commercial, under capitalists of the old type, employing domestic labour and combining commercial and banking activities with the organisation of manufacture. Above all, France remained essentially a rural country and its old agricultural methods continued unchanged.[1] Most statistics in this matter are open to question, but, for what they are worth, the figures for French commerce in 1825, according to Henri Sée, are hardly greater than those of 1788.[2]

This does not entirely settle the question. There is still one final refuge of theory. Capitalist progress during the revolution must not be exaggerated, says M. Soboul. This is rather an under-statement for what seems to have been a period of serious economic decline. However, he continues, the conditions were none the less brought together for the coming great development of capitalist economy.[3] It may seem that this is all a matter of more or less, and that it does not matter fundamentally to what extent the revolution accelerated the growth of a capitalist economy, so long as it did accelerate it. Similarly, the actual effectiveness of corporative restrictions in 1789, and therefore the importance of the legislation of the revolution in liberating trade and industry from

[1] Soboul, *Précis*, p. 441.
[2] *Cf. supra* note 1, p. 74.
[3] Soboul, *Précis*, p. 475.

the bonds of the *ancien régime*, is only a matter of degree. The effectiveness of the abolition of internal customs is perhaps least open to doubt.

All this is on the assumption that the revolution represented a step forward in the direction of a more developed capitalist economy. According to prevailing social theory steps in history must always be taken forward. I want to suggest the possibility that, at least in some fundamental respects, it may not have been a step forward at all, but rather one backwards, that instead of accelerating the growth of a modern capitalist economy in France, the revolution may have retarded it.

As has been said already, the evidence in respect of trade and industry is that France was worse off in 1815 than she had been in 1789. After two decades of war this was perhaps only to be expected. More important is the fact that such evidence as we have on the organisation of trade and industry suggests that by and large it remained in 1815 what it had been in 1789.[1] The lack of capital investment, which had been one of the factors holding back French industrial development, continued. In Dauphiné, says P. Léon, those with capital to invest preferred to the certain risk of losses in industry, the gains of speculation and of investment in real estate.[2] The peasantry, which held so much of the productive capacity of the country, was still largely self-sufficient and invested its savings in land, which attracted capital to the detriment of both industry and commerce.[3] France was

---

[1] For example, in Lyon, Toulouse, Bordeaux.
[2] P. Léon, *La naissance de la grande industrie en Dauphiné* (1954), p. 370.
[3] Crouzet, *op. cit.*, p. 312.

not to know an industrial revolution—apart from isolated and untypical enterprises in a few areas—before the Second Empire. It is true that the economic history of France is largely unwritten. What I am suggesting is that such researches as have been made give no support to the orthodox theory of the economic effects of the revolution, but on the contrary throw great doubt on it. The revolution, in its economic consequences, seems indeed to have been the kind of revolution we should expect if, as has already been suggested, it was led not by industrialists and merchants, but by *officiers* and professional men.

CHAPTER VIII

A BOURGEOISIE OF LANDOWNERS

IT must not be supposed, though Georges Lefebvre did,[1] that I am trying to deny the existence of the French Revolution; I merely want to discover what it was. Professor Reinhard has argued that even if we discard the view that the revolution was against 'feudalism', still the struggle against seigniorial rights, against the noblesse and against the privileged classes was central to it.[2] This may have been true in the summer of 1789. Is it true of the next ten years? Seigniorial rights were largely eliminated in 1789, and their elimination was completed by the stubborn resistance of the peasantry, despite the reluctance of the revolutionary authorities in Paris, in the course of the following years. Similarly, noblesse was legally brought to an end—even if only for 14 years—in 1789, as the marquis de Ferrières philosophically observed on 20 June 1790. 'Noblesse', he writes, 'is already destroyed in fact. The abolition of feudal rights and justice, equality in the division of enclosed land, have given it a mortal blow.' Do not write to me any longer as M. le marquis, he instructs his wife; and let my daughter and son-in-law stop being called count and countess. He even asks for his family arms in the local church to be

---

[1] Lefebvre, 'Le mythe de la Révolution française'.
[2] Reinhard, 'Sur l'histoire de la Révolution française', p. 557.

obliterated, though, since Ferrières was a cautious man, only with whitewash.[1] Finally, privileges based on order, heredity and so on were ended by the legislation of 4–11 August 1789. There was no need, then, to continue the revolution to abolish what had already been abolished.

Yet the revolution did continue, and it continued particularly as a struggle against the 'aristocrats' and 'aristocracy'. This was, it is true, a struggle against the counter-revolution, but that is only to say the same thing in different terms. The counter-revolution was led by, and identified with, the aristocrats; it was also a continuation of that *révolte nobiliaire* against the royal government with which the revolutionary movement had begun in 1787–8, and which had been an attempt to set up or—it was believed—revive, aristocratic government. As such it was a political movement, concerned primarily with political power and only secondarily with social privilege. It is not unreasonable, therefore, to expect the opposition to aristocracy also to be mainly political.

An indication of the primarily political nature of the struggle against aristocracy is the actual use of the word. Tom Paine, writing to Edmund Burke from France on 17 January 1790, explains, 'The term Aristocrat is used here, similar to the word Tory in America;—it in general means an enemy of the Revolution, and is used without that peculiar meaning formerly affixed to Aristocracy.'[2] Nobles could be patriots and if they were such, or often if they were merely discreet and neutral, escaped the label of aristocrats, whereas there were frequent denun-

[1] Marquis de Ferrières, *Correspondance inédite*, p. 212.
[2] *The Correspondence of Edmund Burke*, vol. vi, ed. A. Cobban and R. Smith.

ciations of bourgeois aristocrats, or, to quote Marat among others, of the '*aristocratie d'argent*'.[1] In the Maine, we are told, the term aristocrat was employed to designate even simple peasants if they were hostile to the revolution.[2]

The revolution, then, continued as a political struggle against aristocracy—the claim to a monopoly of political power by a small minority of the nation—when the first objectives had been achieved. This is not to assert that it ceased to have any social aims or content, or to deny that removing from power, wealth, influence, and sometimes even life itself, many members, or whole groups, of the socially superior classes, and replacing them in the end with new men—the '*nouveaux messieurs*', *parvenus*, founders of the 'bourgeois dynasties' of the nineteenth century, was a social as well as a political fact.[3]

How far, apart from the removal of the higher noblesse from their positions of wealth and privilege, there was a permanent change of personnel in the upper ranks of society, however, remains speculative. The bourgeoisie proper of the *ancien régime*, like the noblesse with which it was rapidly becoming assimilated, in some cases survived the storms of the revolution and in some cases went under. The *grande bourgeoisie* of finance, such as the Farmers General, suffered severely, but their place was to be taken by others who differed from them only in being a new first generation of financial wealth, instead of the second or third. The bourgeois who had purchased seigniorial

---

[1] *Cf.* L. G. Wickham Legg, *Select documents of the French Revolution* (1905), I, pp. 171–5.

[2] Bois, *Paysans de l'Ouest*, p. 664, n. 2.

[3] Reinhard, 'Sur l'histoire de la révolution française', p. 561.

dues lost them, but they kept, and probably added to, their estates; and as owners of land profited by the abolition from which they suffered as owners of dues. The bourgeoisie of *officiers*, M. Soboul says, was ruined by the abolition of venality.[1] This is a point which requires investigation. It was an Assembly containing a large proportion of venal officers which carried out the abolition. The abolition was in fact accompanied by compensation and there are indications that the compensation was sometimes profitably invested in the purchase of Church lands. Moreover, many of the former *officiers* seem subsequently to have obtained salaried judicial and administrative positions not dissimilar from those for the loss of which they had earlier been compensated. The open question is how far the expected compensation was actually paid, but even in the upper ranks of the *ancien régime* bourgeoisie it seems likely, that many survived and prospered, or re-emerged after the revolution, to contribute to the recruitment of the new upper class of nineteenth-century France.

Whether many or few survived from the *ancien régime* bourgeoisie is, however, a minor issue. The important question to ask is what essentially was the constitution of the new ruling class of France that emerged from the revolution. I have already suggested that the revolutionary bourgeoisie was the declining one of venal officers, along with members of the liberal professions, rather than the prospering merchants and industrialists.[2] As M. Reinhard puts the point, 'It was these lawyers,

---

[1] Soboul, *Précis*, p. 478.
[2] *V. supra*, ch. vi.

these doctors, these *officiers* of lower positions, who captured the posts of executive power'.[1] For men of business
the revolution was less advantageous: socially and politically they received perhaps even less recognition than
before the revolution. The new Napoleonic élite was one
of soldiers and bureaucrats.[2] Georges Lefebvre truly
writes of Napoleon that he was essentially a soldier: 'His
preference was for an agricultural and peasant society;
the idea of a society dominated by a capitalist economy
was unsympathetic, if not even alien, to him.'[3] The effectiveness of his promotion of the economic interests of
France, it has been pointed out, is an illusion. Though
many historians, and even contemporaries, shared the
belief that the industry of Lyon owed much to Napoleon,
the Lyonnais merchants did not. One, whose correspondence has been edited, is described as having no words too
harsh to use in his criticism of the Emperor and of the
toadyism that his policy encouraged.[4] The tendency,
which Napoleon shared, to look down on business men,
and to exclude them from positions of social prestige or
political power, survived well into the nineteeth century.
As Michelet said, *'La France n'a pas d'âme marchande.'*[5]

If the new ruling class was not constituted out of the
rising industrial or commercial capitalists, then, how was
it composed? Only a few samples have been taken so far,

[1] Reinhard, *op. cit.*, p. 561.
[2] M. Reinhard, 'Élite et noblesse dans la seconde moitié du XVIIIe siècle',
Revue d'histoire moderne et contemporaine, iii (1956).
[3] G. Lefebvre in *Annales historiques de la Révolution française*, no. 119 (1950),
p. 276.
[4] J. Labasse, *La commerce des soies à Lyon sous Napoléon et la crise de 1811*
(1957), p. 31.
[5] Cited in R. Bigo, *Les Bases historiques de la finance moderne* (1933), p. 4.

but these, and all other indications, lead in the same direction. An analysis of the 600 '*plus imposés*'—those in the highest tax grade—of the Haute-Garonne in the year X (1801–2) shows that they included in their ranks former nobles and members of *parlements, officiers*, judges and lawyers, but that the new aristocracy of France was above all one of landed proprietors.[1] 'It has been said', writes the author of this analysis, 'that the First Consul aimed to combine, in the bosom of a new aristocracy, the old noblesse and the industrial and commercial bourgeoisie enriched by the revolution. It seems rather that he aimed to create a new one, whose letters of nobility would be conferred by landed property.'[2]

There can be no doubt that the new ruling class was above all one of landowners. These were the local notables. The basis of their wealth and influence was land, their prime aim to increase these by enlarging their estates. Perhaps Taine saw something fundamental in the revolution when he wrote, 'Whatever the great words— liberty, equality, fraternity—with which the revolution was ornamented, it was essentially a transference of property; that constituted its inmost stay, its prime motive and its historic meaning.'[3] Curiously similar was the verdict of Lefebvre in his earlier, more empirical days. After the abolition of privileges, the nobles and *roturiers* joined, he wrote, in the same social class. The new bourgeoisie was one of '*propriétaires non-exploitants*'.[4]

[1] P. Bouyoux, 'Les "six cents plus imposés" du département de la Haute-Garonne en l'an X', *Annales du Midi*, t. 70 (1958), pp. 317–27.
[2] *Ibid.*
[3] H. Taine, *Les Origines de la France contemporaine: la Révolution* (10th ed. 1881), I, p. 386.
[4] Lefebvre, *Études*, p. 238.

This, of course, is one of those broad judgements which can only be given real substance by much detailed research. It raises a host of questions about the changes in ownership of land during the revolution, which cannot at present be answered. Most of the figures for the possession of land before the revolution are robbed of their significance by one simple flaw. The proportions owned by nobles, peasants, clergy, or others, are usually given as percentages of a whole area. Unless we know also how much is good arable land, how much pasture, and how much marsh, woodland or waste, such figures are practically meaningless. The one statement we can safely make is that the proportions of land owned by different classes varied enormously from one part of the country to another; and this doubtless remained true after, as before, the revolution.

It would be interesting to know to what extent, in different parts of the country, the noblesse kept its lands during the revolution, or regained them after temporary loss. It is said that in many departments of the West the noblesse was able to retain or restore its estates almost in their entirety.[1] We know also that there were many purchases of *biens nationaux* by nobles, sometimes even on behalf of *émigrés*, but we have very little idea what each section of society—aristocracy and upper bourgeoisie, urban middle class, better-off peasants or poorer ones—gained proportionately from their sale.[2] The difficulty of

[1] Bois, *Paysans de l'Ouest*, pp. 313–14.

[2] It is evident that there was great regional diversity in the results of the sales of *biens nationaux*. *Cf.* Lefebvre, *Études*, pp. 235–6. In the Nord, discounting bourgeois purchases from other bourgeois or from *émigrés*, Lefebvre's judgement is that the peasants gained twice as much land as the bourgeois. *Paysans du*

making any reliable estimate is added to by the fact that the initial purchases were often fictitious or speculative, and subsequent sale, especially to peasants, may have changed the whole situation. Whoever they were, many of the purchasers presumably had a sudden accession of wealth through the difference between the nominal and the real price they paid, which resulted from the fall in value of the assignat. We know that wealthy men in the towns purchased a great deal, but we do not know how far the property they kept was urban, and how far rural,

Nord, pp. 504–6. To meet the competition of wealthier purchasers from the towns, the peasants sometimes formed associations to bid for land. C. Porée, *Documents relatifs à la vente des biens nationaux dans le district de Sens* (1912–13), I, p. cxxiii. The decree of 24 April 1793, allowing sale in small lots, and that of 13 September by which the poorer population could acquire the property of *émigrés* up to the value of 500 livres and pay for it by instalments stretched over 20 years without interest, may have assisted peasant purchases. *Paysans du Nord*, p. 462; *cf.* Porée, *op. cit.*, p. xcii. Peasant intimidation may also have played some part in deterring would-be bourgeois purchasers. *Paysans du Nord*, p. 443. On the other hand, business men from the towns are alleged to have formed on occasion a *bande noire* to rig the auctions. Porée, *op. cit.*, p. cxxv. Property in the towns, of course, would not interest the peasants, and here the bourgeois had a monopoly. Lefebvre, *Études*, p. 232. In Sens the bourgeois purchasers, though only 393 in number compared with the peasant 914, acquired twice as much land. At the same time they acquired 114 houses, 9 mills and 21 other buildings to the peasants' 12, 1, and 4 respectively. Porée, *op. cit.*, pp. cxxxii–vi. Round the larger towns in the Nord (and doubtless elsewhere) bourgeois purchases predominated. *Paysans du Nord*, p. 503. Even in the neighbourhood of small towns, like Vire, purchases of *biens nationaux* by peasants were more difficult and rarer. Lefebvre, *Études*, p. 235. The sales of *biens nationaux*, Lefebvre tended to conclude (though not without some doubts and hesitations, for what he says of the Nord seems to indicate the contrary), principally profited the bourgeois. Lefebvre, *Études*, p. 232. In the district of Sens, according to Porée, some small farmers were able to buy land, but the big lots went to the wealthier purchasers. 'Although they sometimes adopted the description of *cultivateurs* then in fashion, they were in reality *bourgeois campagnards*, above all business men, who, having taken the place of the owners in exploiting the domain land and collecting seigniorial dues, were implacable towards the *censitaires*, and had become rich at the expense both of the *seigneur* and of those who owed him their dues or services.' Porée, *op. cit.*, p. cxxii.

since town property is included along with country.[1] Again, did the area of land in large estates, and the number of such estates, increase or decrease? In one department of the West the decline in the number of noble landowners was accompanied by an increase in the size of estates.[2]

How far was the new landed class recruited from its predecessors of the *ancien régime*, and to what extent from new men risen from lower social ranks? Did revolutionary and Napoleonic armies provide entry tickets to the new aristocracy? Was it, to any important extent, a parish-pump aristocracy of local lawyers and business men who seized the opportunity afforded by the troubles of the revolution to accumulate land or houses and promote themselves to the rank of local notables?

Whatever the answers may be to all these questions, the main argument, that this was a revolution which bequeathed to France a ruling class of landowners, remains unaffected. It was, of course, to some extent a different class and type of landowner from that of the *ancien régime*, and one which possessed more political power than its predecessor. If such a class can be called a bourgeoisie, then this was the revolutionary bourgeoisie. If the latter is capable of being interpreted in such terms as these, at least it gives a great deal more sense to the subsequent history of France. We shall not vainly search for a nonexistent industrial revolution, in a country dominated by a landed aristocracy. We shall understand the resistance offered by the landed classes under the Restoration to the

[1] *Cf.* Lefebvre, *Études*, p. 232.
[2] Bois, *Paysans de l'Ouest*, p. 320.

attempt of the *émigrés* to come into their own again—now, unfortunately, too often other people's own. We shall see the bourgeois monarchy of Louis Philippe as what its franchise showed it to be—a government by and for landowners.[1] We shall understand the passionate defence of property by the ruling classes of the nineteenth century and their fear of the great centres of urban population, Paris and Lyon. Above all, it will become comprehensible why a revolution should have laid the foundations of such an intensely conservative society as France was to be for the next century and a half.

---

[1] *Cf.* Sherman Kent, *Electoral Procedure under Louis Philippe* (1937).

CHAPTER IX

COUNTRY AGAINST TOWN

U P to this point I have been discussing the theory that the revolution was the overthrow of feudalism by the bourgeoisie, and trying to restate it in terms which have more regard to the facts of the history of the revolution. This obsolete theory, which was an aid to historical understanding at the beginning of the nineteenth century, has long since become a barrier to it. Above all, it has stood in the way of an appreciation of the real historical conflicts in French society. Since the population of France in the eighteenth century was overwhelmingly rural, one might expect some of these fundamental conflicts to have their roots in rural society; and it should not be too difficult to discover them. There is—it is a safe guess—far more source material available, even in print, on the peasantry than on any other sector of French eighteenth-century society. For the first time, with the revolution, ample documentation for a social analysis of the French countryside exists. Yet, apart from the work of Georges Lefebvre, there had been until the last few years remarkably little research into the problems of rural France. This is perhaps to be attributed, at least in part, to the ideological interests of those who wrote the history of the revolution. It has been written by admirers of the *ancien régime*, who refused to recognise the existence of a peasant problem, by political historians who were not interested in social questions, and by Marxists whose pattern of a bourgeois revolt against feudalism, as I have said above, not only did not allow for any independent action by the peasants, but even prohibited an unprejudiced consideration of their role.

This will seem curious if we remember that it was Marx and Engels who wrote, 'The bourgeoisie has subjected the country to the rule of the towns,'[1] which might be taken as the motto for this chapter. The lesson that they drew was, however, not the one a simple mind might expect. *The Communist Manifesto* continues to praise, not blame, the bourgeoisie, because it 'has thus rescued a considerable part of the population from the idiocy of rural life'. The same bias is evident to the present day. M. Soboul, having allowed that Lefebvre has shown the existence of an autonomous peasant revolution, safeguards the position by adding that of course it was 'in the cadre of the bourgeois revolution'. He continues, to emphasise the same point, 'It is however necessary to underline clearly that the fundamental objective of the peasant movement coincided with the ends of the bourgeois revolution: the destruction of the feudal relations of production.'[2] Why is it necessary, except that the theory requires it? And given the theory, there can really be no object in studying peasant society, except to provide illustrations of what is *a priori* known to be true.

More realistically, in his earlier writings, Georges

[1] *The Communist Manifesto*, 1848.
[2] Soboul, *Précis*, p. 10.

Lefebvre criticised those historians who tended to see the actions of the peasantry as a mere repercussion of the urban revolt, and particularly of that of the 14 July, 'as if the people of the country obeyed the call of the bourgeois'. He insisted on the autonomy of the peasant revolt: up to 14 July, he said, 'the bourgeoisie had neither the time nor the desire to attack the tithe or the feudal rights'.[1] One can go farther. The peasantry was not unaware of the fact that the dues, rights, rents, tithes, services, payments in money and kind, which they felt to be such a great grievance, were often owned, and even more often collected, by the bourgeois. In the years before 1789 the antagonism of the villagers for the towns, the refuge of 'the cowards and the idle', home of the 'capitalists' and their servants, was coming out into the open.[2] It was reflected in the peasant disturbances which, beginning in spring 1789, were not wholly ended by the legislation of 4–11 August. In parts of France, for example Lot and Dordogne, local peasant risings continued into 1790 and 1791.[3] In the Lot, in April 1791, they were no longer directed against nobles, but against the property of bourgeois.[4] Even in 1789 the 'massacre of Ballon', which was responsible for two victims out of the four given by Lefebvre in his *La Grande Peur*, was directed against a rich merchant of Le Mans, recently ennobled, who was attacked *qua* merchant and not as a noble.[5]

Even if only a limited number of attacks on *roturiers* can

[1] Lefebvre, *Études*, p. 249.
[2] Saint-Jacob, *Paysans de la Bourgogne*, p. 559.
[3] Braesch, *1789, l'année cruciale*, pp. 241–3.
[4] Aulard, *La Révolution française et le régime féodal*, p. 135.
[5] Bois, *Paysans de l'Ouest*, p. 164, n.1.

be adduced, the *tiers état* had no doubt that the peasant movement presented a threat to property which must be repressed. Faced with the obvious inability of the royal troops or the *maréchaussée* to restore order in the countryside, they took the defence of property rights into their own hands. They organised the bourgeois militia, or National Guard, the famous *bleus* of the West, sent out troops to protect threatened properties, or on punitive expeditions, and captured, imprisoned, tried and hanged, peasants in considerable numbers.[1] 'The class war was announced', declared Aulard;[2] but this is to ignore the fact that the peasants who had revolted were not the rural poor, or the vagrants who individually or in bands infested the countryside. The *Grande Peur* was rather aroused in part by the fear of these. The last great peasant revolt of France was, as one might have expected, the work of peasant proprietors and tenants. It represented a conflict which is not easily fitted into any pattern derived from the analysis of industrial, capitalist society, but a conflict which must strike any student of the sources who puts preconceived ideas on one side—that between town and country.

Urban resentment at growing signs of rural independence had been shown before 1789. The reforms of July 1787 in local government established assemblies, composed of between 3 and 9 members, in the rural communes. To be elected to these it was necessary to have been domiciled in the parish for not less than one year as well

---

[1] *Cf.* Herbert, *Fall of Feudalism*, pp. 100, 127–8; Lefebvre, *Études*, p. 250; Bois, *Paysans de l'Ouest*, p. 663.

[2] Aulard, *La Révolution française et le régime féodal*, p. 81.

as to pay a minimum annual tax. This meant the setting up of a local government of peasants by peasants and it was greeted with indignant protests from absentee urban proprietors, who were excluded from electoral rights in the villages.[1]

A similar resentment against the granting of political rights to the peasantry was revealed in the elections to the États généraux, when the towns made strenuous attempts to reduce the representation of the rural areas.[2] There was, of course, also the fear that the countryside might be under aristocratic influence. In Franche-Comté, where the privileged orders tried to establish a lower qualification of eligibility for representatives from the country, the *tiers* held out for a higher one.[3] It was

---

[1] Bois, *Paysans de l'Ouest*, p. 659.

[2] The rural demand for representation can be illustrated from the peasant *cahiers* of Artois, which ask for peasants to be admitted to the États. Loriquet, *Cahiers du Pas-de-Calais*, I, pp. 202, 221, 239; and specifically call for the inhabitants of the country to have as many representatives in the États of Artois as the towns. *Ibid.*, I, pp. 181, 275, 512 and *passim*. Alarmed at the numerical preponderance of countrymen among the voters—90 out of every 100 says one *cahier*—the towns wanted the electoral strength of the peasants to be cut drastically to one-half of that of other classes of the Tiers. *Archives parlementaires*, III, p. 493. At Reims it was urged that most of the *tiers état* being peasants it was necessary, in the interests of agriculture, to reduce the numbers of their representatives. A more plausible motive was the fear that the country parishes might elect domestic, textile or metal workers, who would make common cause with workers in the town. Laurent, *Reims et la région rémoise*, pp. 346–7. At Bordeaux, the belief was expressed that malcontents from the town, who had failed to get elected, were going into the villages and country places, stirring up discontent and getting the peasants to choose them as their representatives. Lhéritier, *La Fin de l'ancien régime et la préparation des États généraux*, pp. 227, 229, 232. In the sénéchaussée of Nantes the peasants were able to obtain a majority in the first vote. Patriot protests secured from Necker a drastic reduction in the number of peasant deputies, and in the final elections to the États généraux the eight elected were all Nantais. Soreau, *Chute de l'ancien régime* (1937), p. 138.

[3] J. Egret, 'La Révolution aristocratique en Franche-comté et son échec (1788–1789)', *Revue d'histoire moderne et contemporaine*, I (1954), p. 256.

complained that the rural parishes elected no bourgeois to represent them, but only ignorant *laboureurs*,[1] and that malcontents from the towns were appealing to the vote of the country.[2]

The drafting of the *bailliage cahiers* produced acute conflicts. At Rouen the representatives of the country complained that their views were not represented in the *bailliage cahier*, and violent affrays broke out between them and the town representatives.[3] In their *cahiers* the peasants, given for the first time in centuries the opportunity to express their age-old resentment at the privileges of the towns, did not neglect to use it. 'Peasants are men like any others and should have the same rights,' protested the *cahier* of an Artois village.[4] A *cahier* in Autun describes its small-holders as 'bent over the earth which they water with their sweat, from the rising almost to the setting of the sun, and from which they bring forth by the labour of their hands that produce, that abundance, which is enjoyed by the citizens of the towns.'[5]

Peasant grievances were not confined to such general complaints. Often they were put in quite specific terms, perhaps the most general grievance being of the unequal taxation of the rural population. 'For long', says one *cahier*, 'the hard-working farmers, the strong and worthy *laboureurs*, have groaned equally under the unbearable burden of the taxes. A host of examples proves but too

---

[1] Chassin, *Les Élections et les Cahiers de Paris en 1789*, I, p. 380 (from a pamphlet 'De la nécessité de publier les noms des candidats'); *cf.* Savina et Bernard, *Cahiers de Quimper et de Concarneau*, I, p. 59, n. 1.

[2] *Cf.* Lhéritier, note 260.

[3] Bouloiseau, *Cahiers de Rouen*, I, pp. lxxxviii, civ; II, p. 439.

[4] H. Loriquet, *Cahiers du Pas-de-Calais*, I, p. 184.

[5] Desplaces de Charmasse, *Cahiers d'Autun*, p. 85.

well that the inhabitants of the countryside seem to have been chosen to be the most long-suffering victims of the ills of the nation.'[1] Yet, another says, it is we who feed the inhabitants of the towns.[2] The *cahiers* demand the suppression of taxes which fall only on the country[3] and a removal of the exemptions of the towns.[4] In Auvergne it is complained that Clermont-Ferrand pays only the capitation, and the better-off inhabitants of the country move into the towns to avoid taxation.[5] On the other hand, bourgeois with houses in the country, it is alleged, escape paying the *taille*.[6] Even if the view that the towns got off scot-free was exaggerated, it was widely held, and it is difficult not to believe that it had some substance.

When we begin to look at the social problems of the eighteenth century from the point of view of the peasantry, unexpected angles continually appear. Thus the substitution of a money tax for the *corvée*, instead of being a great reform, turns out to have been a grievance. The fact is at first sight remarkable that *cahiers* are to be found in which the peasantry asks not for the abolition but for the restoration of the *corvée*.[7] The relevant point here is

---

[1] F. Mège, *Les cahiers des paroisses d'Auvergne en 1789* (1899), p. 248.

[2] Loriquet, *Cahiers du Pas-de-Calais*, II, p. 340.

[3] *Ibid.*, II, p. 317.

[4] Bouloiseau, *Cahiers de Rouen*, II, p. 185.

[5] Mège, *Cahiers d'Auvergne*, p. 268.

[6] Bouloiseau, *Cahiers de Rouen*, II, p. 284.

[7] Lefebvre, in his authoritative study of the peasants of the Nord, observed that it was *bien curieuse* that south of the Sambre the villages expressed a preference for the labour *corvée* over the tax which had been substituted for it (Lefebvre, *Paysans du Nord*, p. 236 and n. 2). He offered no explanation and indeed is the only historian who seems to have commented on the fact at all. This is even more curious, because one has only to read some of the volumes of *cahiers* that have been printed to discover that the demand for the abolition of the representative tax substituted for the *corvée* was widespread. It appears,

the complaint of the peasantry that the tax substituted for the *corvée*, which they pay, provides roads that are used by the merchants of the city, who do not contribute to it.[1]

for example, in Autun (Desplaces de Charmasse, *Cahiers d'Autun*, pp. 53, 136), Mirecourt in Lorraine (Martin, *Cahiers de Mirecourt*, pp. 6, 12, etc.), the *bailliage* of Reims (Laurent, *Reims et la région rémoise*, p. 279), and Paris *hors murs* (Chassin, *Les élections et les cahiers de Paris*, IV, p. 468). The Provincial Assemblies in Alsace and in Lorraine, in 1789, favoured the labour *corvée* against the tax (M. Marion, *Dictionnaire des institutions de la France aux XVIIe et XVIIIe siècles* (1923), p. 154), as did the *cahiers* of the *bailliage* of Rouen (Bouloiseau, *Cahiers de Rouen*, II, pp. 300, 319). As late as 1801 the Conseil général of Saône-et-Loire was calling for a restoration of the labour *corvée* (Marion, *loc. cit.*). The failure to take account of this patent fact is yet one more illustration of the effect of theory, elevated to the point of unchallengeable dogma, on the interpretation of the French Revolution. For the abolition of the *corvée* was not only a reform, it meant emancipating labour from customary obligations and putting it freely at the disposal of a money economy. In this way it was an inherent part of the 'bourgeois revolution', and to admit the existence of peasant opposition to it would have been to challenge the essential unity of the revolution. Moreover, it is fairly easy to see that the opposition did not come from the whole rural population but from the better-off farmers, who constitute in the accepted theory the 'rural bourgeoisie', and whose interests were supposed to be identified with the ends of the bourgeois revolution as a whole. If, on the other hand, we forget about the 'bourgeois revolution' and look at the facts it is obvious that the preference in some rural cahiers for the labour *corvée* is not curious at all. The wealthier peasants, wrote an engineer of the *Ponts et chaussées* in 1779, did all they could to prevent the introduction of a tax, reckoning that they were able to have the necessary labour services provided by 'the most wretched class, which is most often dependent on them' (Marion, *loc. cit.*). There were also complaints that sums raised for the *corvée* were not spent on the construction or repair of the main roads (Bouloiseau, II, p. 338). One possible explanation of this is the following. In the généralités of Normandy it seems that the intendants were using road works as a means of providing employment, and to supplement the funds raised by taxation were appealing to the local gentry for contributions. In return the money was spent in constructing or improving the roads to their châteaux. (I owe this information to Dr Olwen Hufton.) There were also the customary demands that all should contribute to the tax, the towns as well as the country (Desplaces de Charmasse, p. 52; Bouloiseau, II, pp. 156, 176, 295); and also that it should be imposed only on those who used the highroads—nobles, rich bourgeois, merchants, carriers, proprietors of diligences—and not on the country people, who, it was said, did not travel on them. (Laurent, p. 279; Bouloiseau, II, pp. 349, 373, 377, 403.)

[1] Bouloiseau, *Cahiers de Rouen*, II, p. 382.

All through the rural *cahiers* there are demands that taxes should be paid by the *gens à portefeuille*, capitalists, merchants.[1] The demand for the abolition of the *octroi* on the entry of articles of consumption into towns is presumably due to the fact that this was paid in the first place by the peasantry on the foodstuffs and drinks they brought in, even if it was passed on to the consumer in increased prices.[2]

All along the line the country-dwellers felt that their interests were sacrificed to those of the townspeople. The Farmers General, they said, substituted for tobacco an 'injurious and corrosive' powder for distribution to the small country *bureaux de tabac*.[3] They asked why peasants should not be able to buy *eau-de-vie* at the same price as nobles, clergy and merchants.[4] Infirmaries only served the poor of the towns and their immediate neighbourhood. 'The unfortunate peasant, without help or resources,' writes a *curé* in reply to the enquiry of 1775, 'has only the choice between beggary and death.'[5] We meet with requests for the rural parishes to be provided with the services of a surgeon, and with schools.[6]

There was a general belief among the peasantry that they were exploited by the bourgeois. 'A swarm of *procureurs* and *avocats*', it was said, descend on the small

---

[1] L. Dubreuil, *Histoire des insurrections de l'ouest* (1929), I, p. 77; Loriquet, *Cahiers du Pas-de-Calais*, I, p. 456; Mège, *Cahiers d'Auvergne*, pp. 320, 348.

[2] Loriquet, *Cahiers du Pas-de-Calais*, I, pp. 154, 217, 326, 454, etc. (see index); Mège, *Cahiers d'Auvergne*, p. 176.

[3] Desplaces de Charmasse, *Cahiers d'Autun*, p. 101; V. Fourastié, *Cahiers de Cahors*, pp. 5, 100.

[4] Savina et Bernard, *Cahiers de Quimper et de Concarneau*, I, pp. 132, 216, etc.

[5] Mège, *Cahiers d'Auvergne*, pp. 145–6.

[6] P. Boissonade, *Cahiers de doléances de la sénéchaussée d'Angoulême* (1907), pp. 397, 424, 426.

towns and villages.[1] Owners of iron-works exhaust the supplies of wood,[2] exploit the forests to the detriment of the peasantry.[3] Even the lawyers engage in economic

[1] C. Étienne, *Cahiers de doléances des bailliages des généralités de Metz et de Nancy* (1912), II, p. 28.

[2] Desplaces de Charmasse, *Cahiers d'Autun*, pp. 245, 246, 248; R. Picard, *Les cahiers de 1789*, p. 55, with references to a large number of *cahiers*.

[3] The exploitation of the forests to the detriment of the peasantry was one of its most general grievances. Wood had been rising in price more rapidly than any other necessity, and as the forests were not let out on a *ferme* the proprietor gained all the increase. Labrousse, *Crise de l'économie française*, p. xxv. The revival and the stricter enforcement of seigniorial rights was also most marked in respect of the forests. M. Duval, 'Économie forestière et féodalité dans l'Ouest à la veille de la Révolution', *Annales de Bretagne*, LXIV (1957), pp. 354–5. Peasant cahiers called for the price of wood to be fixed, *e.g.* Loriquet, *Cahiers du Pas-de-Calais*, I, pp. 162, 204, 248, and *passim*. However, the most general grievance of the peasants was *défrichement*—enclosure and cutting down—of the forests. *E.g.* Bligny-Bondurand, *Cahiers de Nîmes* (1908), I, pp. 267, 360, 457. This robbed the peasants, it was complained, of both fuel and pasture for their beasts, and should be prohibited. Loriquet, *op. cit.*, I, p. 311; II, p. 166.

The case was cited of the destruction of a considerable area of royal forest which had provided Boulogne and its neighbourhood with supplies of wood. In 1780 a private person, on the false pretext that it was of no value and that he would bring in sheep from England and establish a woollen manufacture, had obtained permission to exploit it. Loriquet, *op. cit.*, II, pp. 166, 173. Another common complaint was of the exploitation of the forests to provide fuel for furnaces. *E.g.* Étienne, *Cahiers de Metz et de Nancy*, p. 50 and *passim*. The conflict of interest between the owners of forests and the peasantry is illustrated by the history of the forest of Paimport in Brittany. In the middle of the seventeenth century a small local gentleman had acquired the forest, with the right to establish iron-works (*forges*). The prosperity of these dated from the rebuilding of Rennes after the fire in 1721. The heirs of the founders of the forges rose both in wealth and social status. They acquired offices in the parlement of Rennes and so had support in the courts for their efforts, later in the century, to exclude the peasants from all customary rights in the forest. The beginning of the revolution was marked by agrarian troubles there. A law of 28 August 1792 restored the common rights in the woods, but led to protests by the proprietors. These were upheld by the authorities, who needed the forges for the manufacture of war supplies. The revolution, thus, completed the liberation of the forest from traditional common rights and consolidated the claims of the landed proprietors. M. Denis, 'Grandeur et décadence d'une forêt: Paimport en XVIe au XIXe siècles', *Annales de Bretagne*, LXIV (1957), pp. 264–6.

ventures in competition with the rural population,[1] while, the peasants allege, the towns try to suppress rural industries and to ban the pedlars who serve the countryside.[2] This was certainly true. Round the towns the land worked by the peasants as *métayers* was often owned by the townspeople,[3] and, as has been observed above, they were regarded as harsher landlords than the nobles.[4] An opinion that was widespread in both towns and châteaux, the peasants said, was that 'to be submissive and hard-working, the peasant must be poor'.[5]

Behind all this was the fact that the towns, as the residence of the *'classe propriétaire'*, were the centres of land-ownership. They drained wealth from the surrounding countryside.[6] This has not been an uncommon situation in the history of civilisation. It can be seen today in states building up powerful industrial empires by exploiting a rigidly disciplined, resentful and therefore poorly productive peasantry, as well as in the great civilisations of the past. 'The cities', writes an historian of the Roman

In the Nord, on the other hand, the peasants invaded the woodlands in armed bands to take wood for fuel and building, and to pasture their beasts, in spite of the opposition of the local authorities. In May 1793 the representatives on mission gave them permission to take what they wanted in woods of over ten years' standing. This was equivalent to abandoning all to them. The forests were devastated and it is said that even the roadside trees disappeared. Lefebvre, *Paysans du Nord*, pp. 409–11.

[1] Savina et Bernard, *Cahiers de Quimper et de Concarneau*, I, p. 66.

[2] Picard, *Les cahiers de 1789*, pp. 178, 183.

[3] On *métayage* cf. Lefebvre, *Études*, pp. 163–4, 266; Boissonade, *Cahiers d'Angoulême*, p. 130.

[4] Cf. *supra*, pp. 45–6.

[5] A. F. Le Clerc, *Atlas du commerce* (1786), p. 29: cited in R. Bigo, *Les Bases historiques de la finance moderne* (1933), p. 200.

[6] Cf. M. Vovelle, 'Formes de dépendance d'un milieu urbain, Chartres à l'égard du monde rural', cited in *Annales historiques de la Révolution française*, no. 161 (1960), pp. 351–2.

Empire, 'were economically parasitic on the country. Land was always the best investment, and a community's trade and industry largely depended on the incomes which the urban aristocracies, as absentee landlords, drew from the peasantry. Thus the population of the rustic areas and villages round a town was in most cases reduced to an even lower standard of living than the proletariat within its walls.'[1]

The peasant revolt of 1789, then, far from being a revolt of the bourgeoisie against feudalism, is more realistically treated as a manifestation of the fundamental and age-old conflict of country against town. The legislation of 4–11 August, and the subsequent cessation, first in practice and then in law, of the payment of all seigniorial dues, apparently gave the peasantry what it wanted. It certainly sacrificed the interests of the owners of seigniorial dues to the interests of those who paid them. And, as I have said, the owners of seigniorial rights were often members of the urban middle class so that in this respect it was a revolution against and not for the bourgeoisie. Yet this is not the whole story. If we say that those who profited by the abolition of seigniorial dues were necessarily those who paid them, then this must mean the proprietors, and these also were often bourgeois. In the Sarthe, a recent historian points out, the bourgeois proprietors, owning half the land, were the chief beneficiaries of the reforms.[2]

The picture presented by the abolition of the tithe is similar. Sieyes, speaking against its abolition without

[1] M. Grant, *The World of Rome* (1960), p. 103.
[2] Bois, *Paysans de l'Ouest*, pp. 628–9.

compensation, argued that this would be to despoil the clergy to the advantage of the landowners, 'for each one having purchased his property at a price which discounted the payment for tithe, found himself all of a sudden enriched by a tenth, which was a free present to him.'[1] The laws by which the Constituent Assembly put into effect the abolition of the tithe went farther towards ensuring that the real beneficiary should nearly always be the landowner. In December 1790 it was decided that the owners could claim the equivalent of the tithe in increased rent from their tenants; and in March 1791 the value of the tithe was added to the price of leases concluded before 20 April 1790.[2]

In so far as the bourgeois were landowners, then, and many were, the reforms of 1789 did more perhaps to promote than to injure their economic interests. This did not soften the conflict between country and town. It was intensified by the sale of the *biens nationaux*, the confiscated lands of the church which had been put at the disposition of the nation, and the ensuing competition between town and country for their purchase.[3] Again, to take an illustration from the Sarthe, M. Bois refers to the purchase of *biens nationaux* by urban investors in terms of 'the brutality of the bourgeois intrusion into the countryside.'[4]

After the issue of assignats, and the subsequent inflation, the gulf was dug deeper. The peasants refused to sell their produce in return for rapidly depreciating paper money.

[1] E. Dumont, *Souvenirs sur Mirabeau*, ed. J. Bénétruy (1951), p. 100.
[2] M. Garaud, *La Révolution et la propriété foncière*, p. 253.
[3] Dubreuil, *Histoire des insurrections de l'ouest*, I, 60.
[4] Bois, *Les Paysans de l'Ouest*, p. 657.

The attempt to control prices by the *maximum* antagonised them and discredited the republic in their eyes,[1] while the republicans were indignant at the '*égoïsme aristocratique*' of the peasants. The outbreak of foreign and civil war intensified the conflict by bringing requisitions of carts and horses, wood from the forests, food supplies and fodder, agricultural workers as pioneers for the army, and finally conscription.[2] When the towns, to secure supplies of food at the price fixed by the law of the *maximum*, sent out little expeditionary forces in the form of the *armées révolutionnaires*, the struggle of town and country developed on occasion into open conflict. 'These soldiers, come from Paris', writes Mr Cobb, 'imbued with the mentality of the people of the Sections, found themselves in a countryside abundantly supplied with foodstuffs of all kinds; they brought from Paris a very understandable hostility towards the peasants, an hostility which was largely reciprocated by the latter.'[3]

The conflict of town and country in the West reached its climax in the civil war of the Vendée. This has been made clear recently in articles by Mr Arthur Tilly and in M. Paul Bois' book on the *département* of the Sarthe. At first the revolution appeared to be bringing developments favourable to the interests of the peasants. The first elections in the Vendée, in 1789, gave them control of the local government. This did not last. They were gradually displaced by townspeople between 1789 and 1792, by which time local offices had fallen almost completely

[1] Lefebvre, *Paysans du Nord*, p. 682.

[2] *Ibid.*, pp. 686, 690, 692.

[3] R. Cobb, 'L'armée révolutionnaire dans le district de Pontoise', *Annales historiques de la Révolution française*, no. 119 (1950), p. 217.

under the control of the patriots of the small towns.[1]

It has generally been held that what separated the two sides in the Vendée was the church question; and this has been repeated many times without getting us much farther in the understanding of the revolt. Mr Tilly has pointed out more recently that the strategic questions to ask about the Vendée are not doctrinal but sociological.[2] Here M. Bois comes to our aid. He draws attention to the curious fact that those areas in the Sarthe which most strongly denounced the wealth of the clergy in 1789 were also those which were most violently chouan in feeling a few years later. This apparent paradox is explained by the fact that these were also the districts in which clerical property had been most extensive, and where in consequence the competition of peasants and townspeople for the *biens nationaux* was most acute.[3] In passing, it may be pointed out that the first leaders of the Vendée came from the people—the driver Cathelineau, the game-keeper Stofflet, the wig-maker Gaston, the gabelles-collector Souchu. The nobles only joined in later.[4]

The first battles of the counter-revolution in the Vendée were massive but haphazard forays of the country people against the patriot bourgs and cities. Not a single town, or even simple *bourgade*, took the side of the insurgents.[5] Even the country textile workers, who were despised by the peasant farmers, usually did not join in

[1] C. Tilly, 'Some Problems in the History of the Vendée', *American Historical Review*, LXVII (1961), pp. 28–9.

[2] *Ibid.*, pp. 20–1.

[3] Bois, *Les Paysans de l'Ouest*, p. 658.

[4] Soboul, *Précis*, p. 247.

[5] Bois, *Paysans de l'Ouest*, p. 608.

the revolt.[1] The chouans fought for a variety of reasons, and different factors entered in as the revolt progressed; but basically it represented peasant resistance to the domination of the towns.[2] The enemy for the Vendée was always described as the bourgeois.[3] An earlier historian of the same district, M. Reinhard, described the struggle as one of country against town,[4] and long ago Michelet said the same thing. 'The masses of the people', he wrote, 'sated their old hatred on the *messieurs* of the towns. There [in the Vendée], as elsewhere, the peasant hated the towns under three different heads: as the authority from which came the laws, as bank and industry which drew towards it his money, and finally as his social superior.'[5]

The conflict that assumed its most violent form in the Vendée is not absent from the rest of France; but perhaps I have already said enough to justify the description of one major aspect of the revolution as a revolt of the country against the town.

---

[1] *Ibid.*, p. 621.
[2] *Ibid.*, p. 182.
[3] *Ibid.*, p. 603.
[4] Reinhard, p. 76; *cf.* Bois, p. 601.
[5] Michelet, cited in Bois, *Paysans de l'Ouest*, p. 602.

CHAPTER X

SOCIAL CLEAVAGES AMONG THE PEASANTRY

THE 'country', or the 'peasantry', it must be admitted straight away, is one of those vague formulas, like the 'bourgeois', that are hollow shells, meaningless or misleading unless some concrete content is poured into them. They are general omnibus terms. So long as we recognise them as such they can be harmless and even useful; but they should not be allowed to stand in the way of a closer social analysis. Obviously the peasants are not a single undifferentiated mass, nor is the country a homogeneous unit opposed to the town. The question is, on what lines should its internal cleavages be sought.

Historians have tried to fit the rural population into the Marxist pattern by distinguishing what Lefebvre calls variously a 'rural bourgeoisie',[1] a 'bourgeoisie *campagnarde*',[2] 'bourgeoisie *paysanne des laboureurs*',[3] 'bourgeoisie *rustique*'.[4] To which M. Labrousse adds the descriptions 'bourgeoisie *terrienne*'[5] and 'bourgeoisie *agricole*'.[6] Now undoubtedly among the peasants some were better off

---

[1] Lefebvre, *Paysans du Nord*, p. 34.
[2] *Ibid.*, p. 274.
[3] Lefebvre, *Annales historiques de la Révolution française*, no. 157 (1959), p. 281.
[4] Lefebvre, *Études*, p. 215.
[5] Labrousse, *La crise de l'économie française*, p. xxvii.
[6] R. Mousnier et C. E. Labrousse, *Le XVIIIe siècle* (1953), p. 354.

and some poor to the point of total destitution. But to describe even the former as a bourgeoisie is rather odd. It will be as well to try to discover the composition of this supposed rural bourgeoisie. Here we immediately run into difficulties.

Lefebvre describes his rural bourgeoisie as including two groups: (i) the *grands fermiers*, owning little or no land but deriving a substantial income from their activities as agents, stewards, rent collectors, and so on, for landowners or *seigneurs*; (ii) the farmers or *laboureurs* with holdings of moderate importance.[1] Elsewhere, however, his *grands fermiers* mean the larger farmers, and these are presumably not a component part of the same 'rural bourgeoisie', because we are told that the 'bourgeoisie *paysanne des laboureurs*' gains in numbers and strength as the *grands fermiers* lose land to men on a lower level.[2] It appears, however, from specific studies, that in fact they are not mutually exclusive groups. The large tenant farmer was also often a proprietor of a smaller but still substantial area, and so a *laboureur*,[3] and vice versa. Indeed, unlike Lefebvre, M. Soboul groups the *gros fermiers* (large tenant farmers) along with the *laboureurs* (moderately well-off proprietors) as '*les coqs de village*,' the true 'bourgeoisie *rurale*'.[4] Whether we do this or not, the inclusion of the *grands fermiers* in the first sense—men of business of the *seigneurs*—along with the cultivators,

---

[1] He adds that there were also, living in the country, bourgeois who were not agriculturalists, but these he groups here with the urban bourgeoisie. Lefebvre, *Paysans du Nord*, p. 34, n. 2.

[2] Lefebvre, *Études*, p. 242.

[3] *Cf.* Plaisse, *La baronnie de Neubourg*, p. 554.

[4] Soboul, *Précis*, p. 46.

whether tenants or owners, in the same social group, produces great difficulties for Lefebvre. Of the former he says that they constituted a sort of '*féodalité moderne*',[1] and he opposes them to the latter, the true 'bourgeoisie *rurale*', who were kept out of power by the men of the *seigneur* until 1789, when they took over the leading role in the countryside.[2] On the other hand, for M. Soboul, in another place, the rural bourgeoisie is one which is dominated by notaries and lawyers, who were often seigniorial agents, while the rich *fermiers* (in which sense is not clear, but I think as actual agriculturalists) are excluded.[3] Finally, for M. Labrousse the rural bourgeoisie represents a '*capitalisme foncier*' (meaning large-scale investment in land), which in 1789 seemed to 'industrial society' (what was this, the population of the towns?) the '*fauteur de la vie chère*'.[4] This is even more tailored to an abstract pattern.

If the account of the rural bourgeoisie in the previous paragraph seems somewhat confused, I fear this was unavoidable. With the best will in the world it is impossible to reduce the varying definitions or descriptions of the rural bourgeoisie to sense or consistency. One can only conclude that the idea was invented to fit the requirements of a theory, and to provide the counterpart in the countryside of the urban 'bourgeoisie' and so to explain how peasants also could constitute a bourgeoisie which could join in the overthrow of feudalism.

[1] Lefebvre, *Paysans du Nord*, p. 309.
[2] *Ibid.*, pp. 377–8.
[3] A. Soboul, *Les campagnes montpellérains*, reviewed by E. le Roy Ladurie, *Annales historiques de la Révolution française*, no. 163 (1961), pp. 108–11.
[4] Labrousse, *La crise de l'économie française*, p. xiv.

Further light—or to be honest, further darkness—can be thrown on the idea of the rural bourgeoisie by examining the role which is attributed to it in the countryside. According to Lefebvre and others, it was struggling to abolish *vaine pâture*—the right of commons.[1] This opinion is all the more worth examining because it will enable us to mention a curiously neglected aspect of the agrarian history of France in the eighteenth century—the whole subject of enclosures.

Enclosures is a broad term which covers a number of very different operations—the consolidation of holdings; *défrichement* or draining, clearing and taking into cultivation of areas of waste; abolition of *vaine pâture*—the right of commons; and *partage*—division of the commons between the inhabitants of the *commune*.

In respect of the first of these, the consolidation of holdings, though it was doubtless still proceeding slowly, as it had done in the past and was to continue to do, the revolution does not seem to represent an important phase in its history. It is hardly referred to in the documentation that I have seen. *Défrichement* had also been progressing extensively in the second half of the eighteenth century. Since it was often a means of taking a large area of waste into individual possession it was apt to be resented and during the revolution produced hostile petitions,[2] though there was little success in obtaining the reversal of past enclosures of this type, which was what the petitioners usually asked for. The chief subjects of

[1] Lefebvre, *Paysans du Nord*, p. 412.
[2] *E.g.* G. Bourgin, *Le Partage des biens communaux* (1908), pp. 457, 464–5; Lefebvre, *Paysans du Nord*, p. 222; Sagnac et Caron, *Comités des droits féodaux*, p. 608; Loriquet, *Cahiers du Pas-de-Calais*, I, pp. 62, 204, and *passim*.

controversy during the revolutionary period were neither of these, but rather *vaine pâture* and *partage*.

Edicts allowing the enclosure of commons had been enacted in province after province in the years 1767–71.[1] It was generally favoured by the owners of seigniorial rights, except in Lorraine and Champagne, where they already had the right of *troupeau à part*, which was more advantageous to them.[2] The right of *triage*, by which the owner of the seigniorial rights could take one-third of the enclosed commons, was naturally an inducement to the *seigneurs*.[3] Perhaps it was peasant hostility to *triage* which led the Constituent Assembly, on 15 March 1790, to abolish the right. This decision, if retrospective, would have enabled the peasant communities to re-enter into the possession of communal property of which they had been despoiled. Two months later, on 15 May, however, the Assembly explained that its intention had not been to prejudice actual property rights. On 13 April 1791, when the abolition of the right of *triage* was repeated, the ownership of any lands taken under it before 4 August 1789 was specifically confirmed.[4] Little else could have been expected of what was so largely an assembly of landowners.

Lefebvre's view was that the revolution went much farther than this: it not only sanctioned and aggravated the attacks of the *ancien régime* on collective rights, it extended the authorisation of enclosure to the whole of

[1] G. Lizerand, *Le régime rural de l'ancienne France* (1942), p. 162.
[2] *Ibid.*
[3] S. Herbert, *The Fall of Feudalism in France*, pp. 50–1; *cf.* A. Plaisse, *La baronnie de Neubourg* (1961), p. 561.
[4] G. Bourgin, *Le Partage des biens communaux*, p. viii.

France. It had no regard to the wishes of the immense majority of the peasantry. It had no agricultural policy except to force agriculture into 'the cadres of capitalist production'.[1] M. Soboul puts the same view specifically. The better-off peasants, he says, were hostile to the collective rights which limited their property rights; on the contrary the poor were attached to them because they only survived by their aid.[2]

This is so entirely plausible that it seems almost superfluous to see if it is in accordance with the evidence. Yet there is one generally accepted fact which might have aroused some doubts in the minds of historians if their preconceptions had allowed them to appreciate its significance. This is that, as the revolution moves to the left, instead of diminishing, the pressure for dividing up the common lands increases. An immediate result of the revolution of 10 August 1792 was the legislation of 14 August, which proposed, along with the sale of the property of *émigrés* in small lots, the division (*partage*) of the commons.[3] The object of each of these measures was the same—to attach the poorer inhabitants of the countryside to the revolution, as François de Neufchateau explained.[4] This should at least make us wonder in whose interest *partage* was conceived, as should the strong resistance which the proposals met in the Convention. The decrees of August 1792 only became law on 10 June 1793, when the revolution was approaching its extremest phase. Even then, *partage* was only to be operated if it

[1] Lefebvre, *Études*, p. 260.
[2] Soboul, *Précis*, p. 47.
[3] *L'ancien moniteur*, XIII, p. 419.
[4] Bourgin, *Le Partage des biens communaux*, p. 397.

was voted by at least one-third of the members of the *commune*, and the vital question of the mode of division of the commons was left open. The law, moreover, was of short duration.[1]

The whole matter of *partage* evidently needs closer examination. There are a few documents which attack *partage* allegedly in the interests of the poor; but these are so out of line with most of the documentation as to raise doubts of their sincerity.[2] The ease with which one can be misled on this subject is illustrated by the comment on a document printed as a *glane* (that most tiresome form of antiquarian publication) in the *Annales historiques de la Révolution française*.[3] The comment explains that it is a petition from the '*petits propriétaires montagnards*' of Cantal complaining of the *partage* of the commons as having profited only '*les cultivateurs aisés*'. When we look at the document itself, we find that it is very different. Instead of being small proprietors, its authors call themselves '*les pauvres*', and ask what is to become of them—'*pauvres malheureuses locataires qui n'ont ni bien, ni terre, ni maison pour les loger*'. The petition says that the rich farmers refuse to divide up the commons because they themselves have almost all the benefit of them, with their large herds of cattle. It adds that since the passing of the law ordering the partition of the commons, the rich owners of houses refuse to let them, but leave them empty for fear that their tenants might obtain a share in the commons. In fact instead of being a petition *against* enclosures, it is one *for*

---

[1] Garaud, *La Révolution et la propriété foncière*, pp. 381–5.

[2] Bourgin, *Le Partage des biens communaux*, pp. 75, 269–70.

[3] R. Cobb, 'Plaintes des paysans pauvres du Cantal (nivôse an III)', *Annales historiques de la Révolution française*, no. 163 (1961), pp. 99–101.

them. Thus one has only to read the document itself to discover that it says precisely the opposite of what pre-conceived ideas led its historian to suppose.

There is really very little excuse for the views that are normally expressed on the subject of the peasant attitude to the commons and their enclosure. They cannot survive an examination of the mass of petitions that poured in and were printed by Georges Bourgin in 1908. What do these show? It is clear that there was general agreement that it would be harmful to attempt to divide up mountains and woods into individual ownership.[1] Also, there would have been little point in doing so because they could not provide fields for cultivation. For the rest, two main points emerge from an examination of the petitions. First, the commons were far from being the heritage and resource of the poor: on the contrary there are continual complaints of their exploitation by the flocks and herds of the larger farmers or proprietors.[2] Secondly, it was patently the poorer inhabitants of the country who were in favour of *partage* of the commons, and the better-off ones who were against it. We find repeatedly that it is the landless labourers who petition for *partage*, and the peasant proprietors who are opposed to it.[3] *Partage*, the former say, in petitions of 1792–3, will make the poor into proprietors.[4] They even resort, on

[1] Bourgin, *Le Partage des biens communaux, passim.*

[2] Lefebvre, *Paysans du Nord*, p. 86; Soboul, *Précis d'histoire de la Révolution française*, p. 168; Bourgin, *Le Partage des biens communaux*, pp. 13, 30, 55, 86, 154, 186, 346, 351.

[3] Bourgin, *Le Partage des biens communaux*, pp. 154–5, 159, 160, 162, 172, 311; F. Gerbaux et C. Schmidt, *Comités d'agriculture et de commerce*, I, pp. 389, 390, n.1, 391.

[4] Bourgin, pp. 9, 11, 56, 84, 591, 627.

occasion, to direct action and share out the commons compulsorily.[1] In Lot there was a peasant revolt *for* enclosure in 1791.[2]

On the other hand, the Departmental Directories and General Councils, representing the richer section of the populace, were opposed to it.[3] The peasant proprietors regarded the agitation with great alarm. To give the landless property, they said, was equal to the *loi agraire*—it was communism of property. The proprietors of the canton of Indeville in Doubs, representing, they claimed, five-sixths of all the inhabitants, declared that the right of enjoying the commons had always been inherited along with individual rights of property. 'By what strange principle (other than that of a *loi agraire*)', they asked, 'can a man who has never acquired or possessed anything find himself invested with the exclusive property of a considerable estate, to the prejudice of those who have always enjoyed it?'[4] The *laboureurs* of Saint-Jouy in Haute-Garonne wrote, 'A great number of citizens, deceived and seduced doubtless by those who preach the *loi agraire*, wish to divide up the property of the *ci-devant seigneurs*. It is a crying shame that citizens who have nothing, because they do not like work, should force those who have gained a little property by the sweat of their brow to share the responsibility for their illegal enterprises.'[5]

The Assembly showed that it was not unresponsive to these alarms when it passed the decree of 18 March 1793

[1] *Ibid.*, pp. 411, 461, 464–5, 469, 518, 526–7, 529–30, 532, 540–1, 546–7, 633.
[2] *Ibid.*, p. 396.
[3] *Ibid.*, pp. 2, 3, 9, 37, 59, 126.
[4] *Ibid.*, p. 446.
[5] *Ibid.*, p. 482.

ordering the penalty of death for anyone proposing a *loi agraire*.[1] On the other hand, the *rapport* by Fabre d'Églantine came down strongly in favour of *partage* and even *partage* by head. 'In decreeing the division of the commons', Fabre said, 'the aim of the law was to multiply small proprietors. . . . There are no longer in France nobles, or bourgeois, or boors . . . even domestic servants should share in the division.' He goes so far as to suggest that, without approving illegal distribution of the commons, the division, though illegally made, might be confirmed by a vote of the assembly of the inhabitants and then become lawful.[2]

Finally, the principle of the division of the commons was laid down by a law of 10 June 1793, which a petition from rural '*sans-culottes manœuvriers et autres cultivateurs*' praised for giving '*ces vaquantes immenses*' into 'our laborious hands'.[3] Their rejoicing was premature. The problem, even when the Convention had decided in favour of *partage*, was on what basis the commons should be allocated. Among petitions for division by head, by hearth or family, in proportion to taxation paid, or on a mixture of these principles, the demands for *partage* by head greatly predominated, though its advocates were not always hopeful.[4] Here, for example, is a petition from '*sans-culottes*' of Drôme, on 8 January 1793: 'After 14 August, we will be proprietors, said, with tears in their eyes, our worthy old men to their children. This joy was

[1] *L'ancien moniteur*, vol. XI, 20 mars 1792, pp. 356–7.
[2] Bourgin, pp. 661–88.
[3] Soboul, 'Sans-culottes des campagnes et bourgeoisie rurale', *Annales historiques de la révolution française*, no. 147 (1957), p. 167.
[4] Bourgin, *passim*.

short-lived. Agitators tell them that the Convention will never settle the mode of division.'[1]

In fact, the terms of the law of 10 June were fairly precise. Woods, areas under water, public places and buildings were exempted from partition. Other commons were to be divided up by head of the total population including women, farm servants, *métayers*. Those who shared in the distribution were not to be allowed to alienate their share for the first ten years. How this law was applied, or if it was ever applied, we do not know.[2] Its interest lies not in its results, which were negligible if there were any at all, but in the light which the struggle over *partage* throws on the social structure and stresses of the countryside. In spite of the decision of the Convention, the hopes of the poorer peasants for a share of the land were doomed to frustration. The better-off farmers, the *laboureurs*, kept their hold over the rural communities and it was they who saved the rights of commons. The supposition that as proprietors they must have been in favour of dividing up the commons into individual ownership is one more illustration of the danger of shaping history to fit a theory.

Although he insists on calling them bourgeois (an odd name for peasant proprietors) this view is very close to the opinion of Lefebvre. The '*bourgeoisie du village*' (yet another version of the 'rural bourgeoisie') emerged from the revolution, he says, rich, powerful and numerous,[3] though at the same time the revolution maintained the great landed estates, gains by the bourgeois compensating

[1] *Ibid.*, p. 467.
[2] Lefebvre, *Études*, p. 340.
[3] Lefebvre, *Paysans du Nord*, p. 733.

for losses by the noblesse.[1] Under the Directory, he says, the control of the rural areas passed into the hands of the village *matadors*, this same '*bourgeoisie rurale*'.[2] Matters of terminology apart, there is much in this that the evidence seems to confirm. Yet there is an element of over-simplification, which can be very misleading, in the implication that the peasant proprietors, who were working farmers, and the largely absentee urban landowners, formed one and the same class. In this way the general pattern of the bourgeois revolution is saved, but only by combining under the same heading social groups with radically opposed interests, and at the same time ignoring the basic struggle between town and country that runs through the revolution, and indeed through French history to the present day.

It also involves a fundamental distortion of the agrarian history of the revolution. If the peasant proprietors or farmers are to be grouped with the absentee, urban landowners, clearly they cannot be allowed to have been the protectors of common rights. Hence, since we know that an important part of the common rights of the peasant communities survived the revolution, this fact must be attributed to the resistance of the poorer, landless peasantry. So we have to be told—in the face of documents to the contrary that have been available in print for a generation—that 'the "*petite paysannerie*", deprived of or insufficiently provided with land, was to defend for long its collective rights.'[3] The true picture is

---

[1] *Ibid.*, p. 882; *Études*, p. 242.
[2] Lefebvre, *Paysans du Nord*, p. 674.
[3] Soboul, *Précis*, p. 156.

a very different one. It was the better-off peasant farmers whose stubborn defence maintained the common rights, and whose inherent conservatism, and power consolidated by the revolution, set the pattern of French agriculture and village life for the next century and a half.

CHAPTER XI

THE SANS-CULOTTES

So far I have been considering the interpretation of the revolution as—what indeed it largely was—a revolution of the urban middle classes and the better-off peasantry. The agitation for the partition of the common lands has reminded us that there was also a poorer element in the countryside, and that within the ranks of the peasantry something like a class conflict existed. Cleavages also appeared, though they are perhaps less clearly defined, in urban society. They are revealed in the signs of a proletarian or socialist movement which have been detected behind the bourgeois and capitalist one by socialist historians.

Jaurès was the first to write a 'socialist history' of the revolution, but though he appreciated more of the conflicts in agrarian society than most of his successors, he did not uncover the documentation of the popular movement in the towns. Mathiez went farther, with his discovery of the *enragés*, who combined democratic political ideas with vaguely socialistic economic ones. Though these were easily defeated, he saw the Robespierrist faction of the Jacobins as taking up their policy. Still, however, he hardly penetrated below the middle-class leadership.

A step farther was taken by M. Guérin, who borrowed his description of '*bras nus*' from Michelet, but with a different ideological and social content. He says that his aim was to persuade the workers not to be duped by ideas of class collaboration or of the finality of the French Revolution.[1] Girondins and Montagnards, he insisted, belonged to the same class; they were all bourgeois and fanatical defenders of the rights of private property.[2] Jacobins such as Cambon and Robert Lindet were the protectors of the capitalists.[3] His views have met with bitter criticism from orthodox Communist historians, on the ground, it seems, though this is not actually given as the reason, that he is a Trotskyist. To appreciate the full significance of this, it would be necessary to go into the development of inter-Communist ideological feuds. The non-Communist historian is likely to be impressed with the extent to which orthodox Communist historians have followed M. Guérin in his interpretation of the Mountain and his hostility to Robespierre.

Robespierre, after having been the arch-fiend for most of the historians of the nineteenth century, was suddenly canonised by Mathiez as the saint of social democracy. This, if exaggerated, was an understandable reaction against the former excessive denigration. For the same reason, however, of his social democracy he has been rejected by more recent historians. Thus Robespierrist Ventôse decrees for the distribution in small lots to the propertyless of land confiscated from the *émigrés*, which Mathiez treated as the first step in a new social revolution, and Lefebvre regarded as a sincere if ineffective measure,

[1] D. Guérin, 'Bataille autour de notre mère', *La nouvelle réforme* (1958), p. 196.

[2] Guérin, *Bourgeois et 'bras nus'*, I, p. 100.

[3] *Ibid.*, I, p. 347.

are dismissed by M. Soboul as a mere tactical manœuvre in the general line of the bourgeois revolution.[1]

The ideological element in the writing of history is not, of course, new; but a new ideology can sometimes help in the uncovering of new elements in the past. M. Guérin still remained in fact, although not in theory, on the level of the middle-class revolution, because he confined himself to the printed documentation. Rather unexpectedly, the poorer elements of the rural population emerge in some of the printed sources, while the lower strata of the urban populace remained largely hidden in unexplored archives. More recently, however, revolutionary crowds, *sans-culottes, armées révolutionnaires*, have been extracted from the dusty dossiers of the police and been made the subject of historical treatment.

Dr George Rudé, in his research into the composition of the mobs of the great revolutionary *journées*, soon discovered that the wage-earning class was not a leading element in the working population of Paris and that only slight traces of it are to be found in the political movements of the revolution. The Réveillon riot of 1789, he says, was the only real movement of wage-earners as such in the revolution.[2] This may not be quite correct; but his analysis of the revolutionary crowds correctly refutes the traditional picture of them as composed of hordes of ruffians, the scum of society, drawn by Taine. Professor R. R. Palmer has complained that this was hardly necessary and that Taine is pursued wearisomely by Dr Rudé.[3]

---

[1] Soboul, *Les sans-culottes parisiens de l'an II* (1958), p. 715.

[2] G. Rudé, *The Crowd in the French Revolution* (1959), p. 39.

[3] R. R. Palmer, 'Popular democracy in the French Revolution', *French Historical Studies*, I (1960), pp. 465–6.

This criticism is hardly fair: one prejudice could not be refuted by another prejudice or on a text-book level but only by serious historical research. The positive result of Dr Rudé's analysis has been to show that the revolutionary crowds (as he prefers to call the mobs of the great revolutionary *journées*) were composed of the *menu peuple*—the workshop masters and craftsmen with their journeymen, and the shopkeepers and petty traders of Paris.[1] Individuals from a higher social category—civil servants, *rentiers*, professional men—also joined in.[2] Of course, none, from whatever class he came, was quite typical of it. The street-fighters of the crowds were a militant minority, but they can justly be identified with the *sans-culottes*, says Dr Rudé, because this is a term which, after June 1792, assumes a political connotation.[3] The implications of the term will have to be discussed later. It deserves discussion because whereas *bras nus* is a later literary expression, *sans-culottes* was a contemporary one, and the revolutionaries presumably meant something more or less definite by it.

This brings us to the detailed study of the *sans-culottes* by M. Soboul. He is quite explicit that it is a political term and does not designate a social class. 'A coalition of socially disparate elements,' he says, 'it was sapped by internal contradictions.'[4] 'A patriot and republican bourgeois is freely described as a *sans-culotte*.'[5] Among 343 civil commissaires of the Paris *sans-culottes* in the year II,

[1] Rudé, *op. cit.*, p. 178.
[2] *Ibid.*, p. 184.
[3] *Ibid.*, p. 12.
[4] A. Soboul, *Les sans-culottes parisiens de l'an II*, p. 427.
[5] *Ibid.*, p. 431.

26% lived 'on their property';[1] while the artisans and shopkeepers, who formed the rank and file of the *sans-culottist* movement, marked it with a '*petit-bourgeois*' mentality.[2] Because of the presence of so many small property owners among the *sans-culottes*, they cannot be regarded as embodying a movement of the unpropertied against the propertied classes, in spite of their vociferous hostility to the rich.[3]

One specific manifestation of *sans-culottism* was the appearance of little local *armées révolutionnaires* of ardent patriots. These have been studied in great detail by Mr Richard Cobb. The *armée revolutionnaire* of Paris, he says, included very diverse social elements, though a majority were artisans and shopkeepers.[4] In Bordeaux the local *armée* was joined by some of the wealthier merchants and lawyers.[5] The officers, like the civil *commissaires* of the *sans-culottes*, were of the most varied social origins, and naturally included men of higher status than did the rank and file.[6] Only a minority of wage-earners was included in the Paris *armée révolutionnaire*: hence it could be, and was, used for the repression of movements for higher wages.[7] It is not surprising that Mr Cobb should conclude that the description of the Parisian *armée révolutionnaire* as *sans-culotte* is socially hardly precise.[8]

---

[1] *Ibid.*, p. 442.

[2] A. Soboul, 'Problèmes du travail en l'an II', *Annales historiques de la Révolution française*, no. 144 (1956), p. 240.

[3] *Ibid.*, p. 242.

[4] R. Cobb, *Les armées révolutionnaires* (1961), I, p. 203.

[5] *Ibid.*, I, p. 358.

[6] *Ibid.*, I, p. 55.

[7] *Ibid.*, I, p. 47.

[8] *Ibid.*, I, p. 54.

A study of the *sans-culottist* movement in the post-Thermidorean period by the Norwegian historian, Mr K. D. Tønnesson, does not help to clarify the problem of its social composition. He defines the *sans-culottes* as those members of the *menu peuple* taking revolutionary action.[1] This is to exclude many known *sans-culottes* who were not *menu peuple*; and it hardly avoids the difficulty to say that these leaders came from the '*couches supérieures*' of the *sans-culottes* on the confines of the bourgeoisie.[2]

M. Soboul, the chief historian of the *sans-culottes*, frankly recognises that the term is vague in relation to the actual sociological vocabulary of the present day; but, he adds, 'in relation to the social conditions of the time it corresponds to a reality'.[3] When we ask what this reality was, we may not be quite so happy, especially as he himself has told us elsewhere that *sans-culottism* was a combination of socially disparate elements. 'Privilege, landed wealth, seigniorial rights, in short all that characterises a still feudal society', writes M. Soboul, 'that is what, in the person of the *aristocrat*, the *sans-culotte*, whether he is a worker or a peasant, rises up against.'[4] This is eloquent, indeed moving, but does it provide us with a social definition? The ghost of feudalism once more reappears to haunt our discussions, only instead of being the bourgeois who are defined in terms of their enmity to feudalism it is now the *sans-culottes*. Oddly enough, the bourgeois seem to have faded out of the picture, in fact almost to have become identified with the aristocratic

[1] K. D. Tønnesson, *La défaite des sans-culottes* (1959), p. xviii.
[2] *Ibid.*, p. 358.
[3] Soboul, *Les sans-culottes parisiens*, p. 454.
[4] Soboul, 'Problèmes du travail en l'an II', p. 241.

enemy. Yet the one element of unity among the *sans-culottes*, hostility to the aristocrats,[1] was also the element which had united the bourgeois.

The explanation, in this case also, is that the *sans-culottes*, like the bourgeois, are not a social class; they are defined essentially in political, and not in social, terms. The primarily political aims of the *sans-culottist* leaders were illustrated on 4–5 September 1793, when Chaumette and Hébert diverted the agitation of workers for a general maximum into political channels.[2] Mr Cobb also treats the *sans-culottes* as a political and not a social category. Indeed, socially they are hardly to be distinguished from their enemies of the federal revolts. For instance, at Lyon the federal army included the populace of the sections. True, it could be said that the federalist armies were the instrument of groups of higher social position than their average members,[3] but the same was also true of the *sans-culottist* movement.

This political interpretation of the *sans-culottes* is a curious reaction from earlier socialist interpretations of left-wing movements in the revolution. Dr Rudé similarly emphasises that his revolutionary crowds were politically motivated and not inspired merely by short-term economic ends.[4] Throughout the revolution, he says, the *sans-culottes* identified themselves with a wide range of political aims.[5] This does not mean that they produced these aims themselves, or even that the leaders

---

[1] Soboul, *Les sans-culottes parisiens*, p. 473.
[2] *Ibid.*, p. 168.
[3] Cobb, *Les armées révolutionnaires*, I, p. 49.
[4] Rudé, *The Crowd in the French Revolution*, pp. 207–8.
[5] *Ibid.*, p. 207.

who expressed them belonged to the same class socially. The leaders were drawn from the higher ranks of society,[1] and without the impact of the ideas provided by these leaders, it is frankly admitted, the popular movement would have remained powerless and barren.[2] Their ideas were conveyed to the *sans-culottes* by agitators, secondary leaders like Fournier, Maillard, Saint-Huruge, Saint-Félix, Théroigne de Mericourt, Claire Lacombe—a curious list;[3] by pamphlets and journals in popular language;[4] by indoctrination in the National Guard, clubs and sections; by argumentation in public meetings and wine-shops.[5]

The extent to which the rank and file of the *sans-culottes* were in fact indoctrinated with political ideas by their social superiors must remain speculative for lack of positive evidence. Dr Rudé relies rather too much on the circulation of a few political slogans—and one knows how easily a crowd can be taught to chant these and how little serious political content they can have. It is suspicious also to find him citing repeatedly a single specific case—that of the cook, Constance Evrard, who at her examination declared indignantly that she knew how to read, and had read Prudhomme, Marat, Desmoulins—as the one living piece of evidence for his argument, except in the index where she is omitted.[6]

Lefebvre shrewdly pointed out that if what united the

[1] *Ibid.*, p. 172.
[2] *Ibid.*, p. 209.
[3] *Ibid.*, pp. 190, 239.
[4] *Ibid.*, p. 211; Soboul, *Les sans-culottes parisiens*, p. 160.
[5] Rudé, *The Crowd in the French Revolution*, pp. 212–15.
[6] *Ibid.*, pp. 86–7, 190, 197, 212.

sans-culottes was their political ideas, then these did not distinguish them from the Mountain, the policy of which, he argued, could be regarded as opposed to the social interests of its own class.[1] M. Soboul's way out of this difficulty is to challenge the motives of the Mountain. 'Without raising the question of the sincerity of the Robespierrists', he says, though this in fact is what he is doing, 'there was in such a policy a tactical necessity.'[2] His much severer criticism of the motives of the *sans-culottist* leaders does not seem to worry him. He does not pretend that they were disinterested.[3] Hébert was 'inspired by ambition and anxious to preserve his popular clientèle',[4] Vincent 'cross-grained and vindictive'.[5] Lacking the oratory or political culture of the Jacobins, the *sans-culottist* militants, we are told, could only control the assemblies of the sections by denunciations, purges, fraud, and paying their supporters.[6] There was a struggle among them for jobs.[7] Hébert's denunciation of Roux and Leclerc on 8 September was an intrigue inspired by jealousy of their influence.[8]

In addition to this frank admission of the contemptible character of the *sans-culottist* leaders by those who nevertheless choose them as their political heroes, the followers, the *menu peuple*, are admitted to represent a class which

---

[1] G. Lefebvre, review of Soboul, 'Les sans-culottes parisiens' in *Annales historiques de la Révolution française*, no. 156 (1959), pp. 171–2.

[2] Soboul, *Les sans-culottes parisiens*, pp. 418–19.

[3] *Ibid.*, p. 139.

[4] *Ibid.*, p. 142.

[5] *Ibid.*, p. 354.

[6] *Ibid.*, p. 361.

[7] *Ibid.*, p. 697 n.

[8] *Ibid.*, p. 322.

Marxism condemns without reserve. 'The lower middle class, the small manufacturers, the shopkeeper, the artisan, the peasant', says the *Communist Manifesto*, 'all these fight against the bourgeoisie, to save from extinction their existence as fractions of the middle class. They are therefore not revolutionary but conservative. Nay, more, they are reactionary, for they try to roll back the wheel of history.'[1] How, in the light of all this, is the fascination of the *sans-culottist* movement for contemporary Communist historians, and their obvious sense of kinship with it, to be explained?

A clue to the answer is given by the distinguished historian of the Bolshevik Revolution, Mr E. H. Carr. He points out, first, that the names which historians use to describe the Paris crowds—*les sans-culottes*, *le peuple*, *les bras nus*, *la canaille*—'are all, for those who know the rules of the game, manifestos of a political affiliation and of a particular interpretation';[2] and secondly, that the current Communist theory is not Marxism but Marxism-Leninism.[3] A brief summary of the latter will reveal at once its relevance to the contemporary historiography of the French Revolution.[4]

Lenin, it must be premised, was preoccupied with the problem of seizing power, that is, he was absorbed in political problems *per se*; and this in a society with a low level of industrialisation and without a numerically strong working class. In these respects Russia in 1917 and

[1] *The Communist Manifesto* (1848).
[2] E. H. Carr, *What is History?* (1961), p. 19.
[3] *Ibid.*, pp. 132–3.
[4] For the following account I am indebted to A. G. Meyer, *Leninism* (1957). See especially pp. 29–33, 47, 108.

France in 1789 offer obvious parallels. For Lenin the working masses, because of the conditions under which they live, have a spontaneous impulse to revolt. However, this is ineffective by itself unless it is brought to consciousness (not, as in Marx, class-consciousness). The consciousness, which the workers lack, is possessed by an élite of bourgeois intellectuals, whose function it is to assume leadership of the spontaneous movement of the working classes. The instrument of their leadership is the political party, which by a combination of propaganda and coercion induces the proletariat to accept its leadership. When the conscious élite seizes power, this is the proletarian revolution.

In the light of Leninist theory it becomes possible to understand why the *sans-culottist* movement, along with the later *babeuvist* conspiracy, constitute the chief interest in the French Revolution for modern Communist historians: these movements can be regarded as a dress rehearsal for the Leninist revolution. Hence the enormous concentration of attention on what were, after all, only transient episodes, which left little permanent mark on the evolution of French society. Hence, too, the loss of interest in the *enragés*. There is nothing in Jacques Roux, says the East German professor, W. Markov, beyond the idea of direct democracy, which is common to all the *sans-culottes*.[1] Hence, too, above all, the remarkable decline of interest in the economic history of the revolution. Earlier, Marxism stimulated research into the economic conditions of the revolution, though its rigid

[1] W. Markov, 'Les "Jacqueroutins"', *Annales historiques de la Révolution française*, no. 160 (1960), p. 181.

pattern and inadequate terminology prevented that research from achieving the results it otherwise might have done. Leninism diverted attention from conflicts based on economic motivation to the political struggle for power, and since the revolution was so largely a struggle for power, recent Communist historians have been able to make important contributions to its history. On the other hand, both Marxism and Leninism, by reducing the economic and political conflicts in society to stereotypes, have tended to prevent them from being appreciated in their full acuteness or complexity. This criticism must not be taken to imply that any other historians of the revolution had been free from ideological presuppositions, or that the more recent ideological influences have not been of use in directing attention to neglected aspects of the history of the revolution and in stimulating research. The political history of the revolution has gained; but for the same reason, for the social historian of revolutionary France, the *sans-culottes* have been almost literally a red-herring to divert attention from the basic social problems, both rural and urban, of French Revolutionary history.

CHAPTER XII

A REVOLUTION OF THE PROPERTIED CLASSES

THE attention of general revolutionary historians has all along been directed primarily to political conflicts. This is not unjustifiable, because those who guided the revolution in Paris, and whose rivalries make up its history, were politicians. By and large they all shared the same basic economic and social ideas. Once the struggle against the privileges of the noblesse was over, in 1789, the revolution became a political conflict, waged for the government of France. The question is whether there was a class conflict beneath this.

There is no sign, it has been said, of such a conflict in the *cahiers* of 1789.[1] This may mean that there was no such conflict, or that evidence of it has not been found, and if it has not been found this may be because it has not been looked for. I have already suggested that the evidence for agrarian social conflicts was not far to seek. Nineteenth-century 'bourgeois' historians, imbedded in the theory of political democracy, were not likely to detect a conflict of economic interests within the ranks of the 'people'. More recently, historians with a stronger economic interest have rightly refused to see the class divisions of modern times in the pre-industrial society of eighteenth-century

---

[1] Picard, *Les cahiers de 1789*, p. 267, cites Babeau, Du Cellier, Jaurès and C. Bloch to this effect. He himself challenges its correctness.

France. Also, the natural tendency is to look for evidence of social conflict primarily in the form of movements from below. As I hope to show, signs of these were not lacking in the France of the revolution, but priority should be given to what was possibly a stronger sentiment and certainly one which received more articulate expression—the evidence of a class war from above, the fear and resentment of the better-off sections of society against the poor.

The pressure of the unpropertied populace on those with property and social position was something which respectable society was becoming acutely conscious of in the eighteenth century. Its basic cause, indeed the dominating fact in eighteenth-century France, was the great rise in population, perhaps from some 15 millions at the beginning of the century to 26 at the end. Admittedly all such figures, before the nineteenth century, are speculative, but there can be little doubt that there was a substantial growth, both actual and proportional, in population, and along with this a great increase in the numbers of the poor—the landless, craftless, statusless workers in both country and town.[1]

The increase in the numbers of the poor was alarming to respectable society and not without reason. An examination of the *taille* lists for 1785 in 22 parishes in the neighbourhood of Caen, taking the assessment of 5 livres as the poverty line, has shown that nearly half the total population did not reach this figure.[2] Camille Bloch

---

[1] *Cf.* Lefebvre, *Paysans du Nord*, pp. 57–8.

[2] F. Fournet, *La population du district de Caen sous le règne de Louis XVI*, pp. 32–3. I owe this reference to Professor Alun Davies.

argued that it was not possible to estimate the numbers of the poor or the degree of their poverty, but more recently evidence has been dug out which suggests that this was an unduly pessimistic view.[1] M. Bouloiseau has used for the region of Rouen an enquiry by the *Commission intermédiaire* of the Provincial Assembly on pauperism, and a list of heads of families assessed to the *taille*, for the purpose of estimating the numbers of the poor. Out of 16,548 households, it appears, some 2,530 can be counted as indigent, that is a minimum of 14% of the populace, though this M. Bouloiseau believes to be much under the real figure.[2] A considerable proportion of the indigent were, of course, women and children, as well as the old and infirm.[3] The flood of children abandoned by their parents completely swamped the resources of local foundling hospitals in spite of the high death rate in these. The government had to prohibit the convoys of foundling babies sent off to Paris, where, although many perished *en route*, the foundling hospital could not cope with those who survived the journey; but local authorities disregarded the prohibition.[4]

The lists of *mendiants*—beggars—have, of course, to be read in the light of *ancien régime* conditions and the tradition of the Roman Catholic church, in which charity was a duty of the faithful and beggary an honourable station in life. One parish in the Nord in 1790 possessed 12 professional beggars. Often, says Lefebvre, it was an

---

[1] Bouloiseau, *Cahiers de Rouen*, I, p. cxxxix.
[2] *Ibid.*, I, p. cxlviii.
[3] *Cf.* Lefebvre, *Paysans du Nord*, p. 298.
[4] I take these statements from Dr Olwen Hufton's study of the town of Bayeux.

hereditary profession passed on from father to son.[1] Un-expectedly, one finds in the tax lists the assessments of professional beggars. In 1790 Douai had 26% classed as indigent but only 11% exempt from taxes.[2] Beggars are even found on the lists of the Patriotic Contri-bution.[3]

The obligation of charity to beggars was not one which was welcomed by the farmers and smallholders. Because of the increasing numbers of the poor, the burden was becoming heavier and was bitterly resented. When by his improvidence anyone is ruined, says a Norman *cahier*, it is always the farmer to whom he looks for his support.[4] The whole nation should be responsible for the relief of the poor, it was claimed: the farmers and country-people cannot continue to support them.[5]

The poor were not only a financial burden, they were a daily, and even more nightly, threat. They demand their alms with insolence, and are sure of getting what they demand, says a *cahier* of Autun, because the farmers have straw and hay which is threatened with arson by vaga-bonds if they do not get what they want.[6] They exact their contributions by threats:[7] begging easily turns into pillage.[8] The '*sommeurs*', as the able-bodied beggars who employed menaces were called, were subjected to heavy

---

[1] Lefebvre, *Paysans du Nord*, p. 298.
[2] *Ibid.*, p. 293.
[3] *Ibid.*, p. 298.
[4] Bouloiseau, *Cahiers de Rouen*, II, p. 239; *cf.* Lefebvre, *Paysans du Nord*, p. 299.
[5] Loriquet, *Cahiers du Pas-de-Calais*, I, p. 224.
[6] Desplaces de Charmasse, *Cahiers d'Autun*, pp. 42, 119, 193.
[7] *Ibid.*, p. 110; Loriquet, I,.p. 205; Bouloiseau, *Cahiers de Rouen*, II, p. 244.
[8] Lefebvre, *Paysans du Nord*, p. 249.

penalties by the wheel or fire in the attempt to suppress them, but unavailingly.[1]

There were deep feelings involved in the attack on the practice of begging. It expressed the profound antagonism of those with property against 'that élite of paupers which begins by begging and ends by stealing'.[2] Begging, say the grocers of Rouen, has attractions for the lazy, and many of those who make a profession of it would be unwilling to forsake a means of existence which they regard as '*une propriété*'.[3] The wine and cider sellers of the same town say that begging is against the natural law.[4] The *cahier* of Fuges in Cahors denounces 'that spirit of disorder, of independence, of roguery, of rapine and theft' which infects the lowest class of the people. Parents, it says, train their children as beggars, the children become insensibly accustomed to idleness, and from that it is only one step to debauchery and crime; grown up, they make honest men tremble on their own hearths.[5] Such complaints need not be regarded as insincere, though it is a somewhat suspicious circumstance to find them joined with the complaint that as a result of the spread of begging, '*les gros laboureurs, les gros propriétaires*' are without sufficient man-power for the cultivation of their land, and so find it difficult to pay their taxes or even to survive.[6]

The attitude to the problem of poverty that appears in

---

[1] *Ibid.*, pp. 300–1.
[2] F. Mège, *Cahiers d'Auvergne*, p. 338.
[3] Bouloiseau, *Cahiers de Rouen*, i, p. 152.
[4] *Ibid.*, p. 125.
[5] V. Fourastié, *Cahiers de Cahors*, p. 118.
[6] *Ibid.*, p. 119.

the *cahiers* is mostly a negative one. The foundation of infirmaries, says a *cahier* from the Pas-de-Calais, will only multiply debauchery and excesses, because where they exist one hears the poor say, 'We risk nothing in drinking and enjoying ourselves, since in any case we can go with our children to the poor-house.'[1] A widespread demand is for a settlement law, compelling paupers to remain in the parish in which they have their domicile,[2] and making each parish responsible for its own poor.[3] Sometimes the building of a poor-house is suggested.[4]

The mixture of fear and enmity with which the poor were regarded by those above them in the social scale appears also in the attitude to the day-labourers, who also might easily have, at least for part of the year, to live on charity. 'The manual worker, naturally improvident', says a *cahier* of Vermentois, 'having nothing to induce him to save, becomes less anxious for work and soon falls into idleness.' Its solution is to impose the tax of the *vingtième* on his wages.[5]

In the election campaign for the district of Filles-saint-Thomas in Paris, Brissot, that voice of the Girondin upper bourgeoisie as we are told *ad nauseam* and without evidence, protested against the slandering of the people, 'or at least that part of the people which lives on independent labour, the artisans'. It was not these who caused the disturbances in electoral meetings, he said, but the clerks,

---

[1] Loriquet, *Cahiers du Pas-de-Calais*, I, pp. 144–5.
[2] Fourastié, p. 297; Desplaces de Charmasse, p. 23; Bouloiseau, *Cahiers de Rouen*, II, pp. 112, 132, 239.
[3] Desplaces de Charmasse, p. 26 and *passim*.
[4] *Ibid.*, pp. 323, 382; Bouloiseau, II, pp. 23, 240; Fourastié, p. 297.
[5] Picard, *Les cahiers de 1789*, p. 217.

valets and other dependents of the rich and powerful. Of course, he added, this was not the view of the *haut tiers*, which had even more contempt for the people than the noblesse had.[1] Very few contemporaries went as far in recognising economic facts as one Breton noble, who said that the real inequality was not between noble and *roturier* but between rich and poor;[2] or a former curé from Auvergne, who, in 1790, asked what the *tiers état*, when it had raised itself to the level of the nobles and the clergy, would say to the artisans and the people who demanded to be raised to *its* level. 'Remember', he wrote, 'that your pens are less to be feared than the swords of the nobles, your speeches are less respected than those of the priests, and your houses will offer less resistance than the châteaux'[3]—but in all this he was very mistaken.

The fear of the people on the part of the respectable classes is again illustrated in the *cahiers* by the attacks on 'cabarets'—inns or wine-shops. They were, it was said, a source of debauchery and idleness, the ruin of day-labourers and their families.[4] In them thefts were planned and brigandage grew up.[5] All should be closed, except in towns or within a quarter of a league of the main high-ways; and they should only be allowed to supply travellers, not the local population.[6] We may suspect

[1] Chassin, *Élections et cahiers de Paris*, II, p. 402.

[2] H. Sée, *Cahiers de Rennes*, I, p. xli.

[3] Rouganne, 'Observations réfléchies sur différentes motions de M. l'Évêque d'Autun, 1790'. *Annales historiques de la Révolution française*, no. 135 (1954), pp. 177–8.

[4] E. Bligny-Bondurand, *Cahiers de doléances de la sénéchaussée de Nîmes*, I, p. 34; Fourastié, p. 150; Bouloiseau, II, p. 119 and *passim*.

[5] Bligny-Bondurand, I, p. 34; Fourastié, p. 318.

[6] Fourastié, p. 267; Bouloiseau, II, pp. 156, 167 and *passim*; Savina et Bernard, *Cahiers de Quimper et de Concarneau*, I, p. 256.

something more than the professed desire to protect morality and the interest of the family in the attack on inns and taverns. The day-labourers met at the inn and discussed public affairs over a glass of *eau-de-vie*, declared the Norman *cahiers*. Perhaps this was one reason why a majority of the parishes of Normandy called for them to be closed.[1] Later, not only were they deplored as the resort of violent and criminal elements, they were also feared as centres from which revolutionary ideas were propagated.[2]

Another example of the social stresses in the countryside may be seen in the attacks on the traditional right of gleaning, denounced by the noblesse in the Boulonnais as the occupation of men '*sans foi comme sans honneur*',[3] and by the *tiers* as the profession of do-nothings and pillagers.[4] Severe penalties were called for on able-bodied persons who took to gleaning instead of honest work.[5] Petitions from the poorer population showed that this was not merely an attack in theory. Gleaning, claimed the inhabitants of Forceaux in Eure, was 'the patrimony of the poor.'[6] Petitions of 1790 professed that the farmers were sending their farm-servants out into the fields immediately the corn was cut, and even before dawn, to rob the poor of their traditional right.[7]

---

[1] Bouloiseau, 'Élections de 1789 et communautés rurales en Haute Normandie', *Annales historiques de la Révolution française*, no. 142 (1956), p. 42.

[2] Cobb, *Les armées révolutionnaires*, I, pp. 156–7.

[3] Loriquet, *Cahiers du Pas-de-Calais*, II, p. 105.

[4] *Ibid.*, II, p. 179.

[5] *Ibid.*, II, p. 187.

[6] Gerbaux et Schmidt, *Procès-verbaux des comités d'agriculture et de commerce*, I, p. 498.

[7] *Ibid.*, I, pp. 478, 512.

Finally, it is odd to find, in a period of intense rural over-population and under-employment, complaints of the flight of labour to the towns, and of rural depopulation, but we do find these.[1] An excessive love of money, it is said, attracts the poor to the towns.[2] Corrupted from the earliest age, young people desert the country and flock to the towns 'to give themselves over without restraint to all kinds of vice'.[3] Thus agriculture is robbed of the labour that it needs.[4] For the same reason—that of robbing agriculture of labour—there are complaints against the Cherbourg harbour construction and the mines.[5] One suggested remedy was a tax on those who took labour from the countryside,[6] and one on male servants, 'in order to leave this class of men to agriculture, for which it was born'.[7]

Similar social tensions may also be seen in the towns, for example in demands for the suppression of the *monts-de-piété*. These had been founded in 1777 and may be counted among the social reforms which marked the last phase of the *ancien régime*. The aim, according to Necker, was 'to relieve the subjects of the King in their family affairs, and to help business men to avoid the shame and injury of distraint'.[8] In 1789 there were 194 officials and 600,000 articles pledged, at an interest of 10%, in the *monts-de-piété*. It was said that they recruited

---

[1] Boissonade, *Cahiers d'Angoulême*, pp. 259, 275.
[2] Bouloiseau, *Cahiers de Rouen*, II, p. 236.
[3] Fourastié, *Cahiers de Cahors*, p. 12.
[4] Boissonade, p. 275; Fourastié, p. 150; Desplaces de Charmasse, p. 22.
[5] Picard, *Les cahiers de 1789*, pp. 111-12.
[6] *Ibid.*, p. 177.
[7] Bligny-Bondurand, *Cahiers de Nîmes*, I, p. 443.
[8] R. Bigo, *Les Bases historiques de la finance moderne*, p. 73.

their clients among the better off, but the great majority of the articles pledged were under 24 livres in value,[1] and the attacks on the institution suggest that they were more used by the lower sections of urban society. They were attacked widely in the Paris *cahiers* by clergy,[2] nobles[3] and *tiers état*.[4] It was complained that their interest was usurious,[5] that they served as a means of disposing of stolen articles and assisting fraudulent bankruptcies.[6] Perhaps more to the point were complaints that they injured commerce and manufacture,[7] presumably by the sale of unredeemed goods. A curé alleged that the watchmakers were being ruined by the sales of the *monts-de-piété*.[8] Suppressed by the Convention in the year IV, they were re-opened under the Directory,[9] which is some evidence that they served a useful purpose.

The final test of the contempt of the *tiers* for the people, to use the eighteenth-century terms, came with the introduction of the institutions of political democracy. Long before 1789, the relics of popular representation in local assemblies had disappeared. In 1733 the *sous-délégué* of Bar-sur-Aube, for example, asked for the suppression of an electorate composed of 'more than four hundred vine-growers, workmen and artisans', who, he said, had kept the syndic in office despite royal edicts to the contrary and

[1] *Ibid.*
[2] Chassin, *Les Élections et les cahiers de Paris*, II, pp. 37–8; III, p. 310.
[3] *Ibid.*, II, p. 288.
[4] *Ibid.*, II, pp. 410, 428, 454, 455, 476, 479, 522; III, pp. 404–5; IV, p. 159 (Versailles).
[5] *Ibid.*, II, pp. 37–8; III, pp. 404–5.
[6] *Ibid.*, II, p. 410; III, pp. 404–5.
[7] *Ibid.*, II, pp. 410, 476, 522, 532.
[8] *Ibid.*, II, p. 548.
[9] Bigo, p. 74.

the orders of the intendant.[1] Among many other measures may be named the edicts of 1764 and 1765, substituting for elections local councils of notables.[2] The assembly of Rennes was suppressed in 1766, the intendant complaining that it contained 'many artisans with no idea of the principles and rights of the municipality'.[3] In 1784 the intendant of Burgundy wrote that many of the towns in his *généralité* had realised 'the inconvenience of assembling all the inhabitants'. These assemblies, he said, 'where the least docile citizens silence those who are wise and educated', were a source of disorder.[4]

Examples only need be given of the limited views of the *tiers état* on the desirable scope of a democratic franchise. A petition of December 1788, drawn up on behalf of 'domiciled citizens of Paris' by the famous Dr Guillotin and adopted by the Six Corps, called for exclusion from the electoral assemblies of '*hommes non domiciliés*', because they were not really free and were dependent on others.[5] A memoir signed by 108 Parisians proclaimed, 'It must be recognised that there is a class of men who, by the nature of their education and the kind of work to which they are doomed by their poverty, are equally devoid of ideas and will-power, and incapable, at present, of taking part in public business.'[6]

Such precautions were hardly needed. The poorer Parisians stayed away from the electoral assemblies, either

---

[1] A. Babeau, *La ville sous l'ancien régime* (1884), p. 72.
[2] *Ibid.*, p. 62.
[3] *Ibid.*
[4] *Ibid.*, p. 60.
[5] Chassin, *Cahiers de Paris*, I, p. 40.
[6] *Ibid.*, I, p. 91.

by being excluded or of their own choice.[1] In Rouen many small artisans were unwilling to lose their day's work to attend the electoral assembly.[2] Where they did attend, they usually found that little attention was paid to their wishes. In a Rouen electoral assembly where the poorer inhabitants were present, finding that their grievances were not reflected in the *cahier*, they refused to sign it, 'crying out that common bread cost 3s. 6d. the small loaf'.[3] In Reims, one Hédoin de Pons-Ludon, a retired army officer who had quarrelled with the authorities, supported the workers in the hope of gaining the popular vote. The town council had decided that all inhabitants who were not members of a corporation might meet at the hôtel de ville to draw up a *cahier* and elect representatives. Hédoin led a large body of workers there but they failed to maintain their claims. 'The repression of the poor class at Reims in March 1789, the exclusion from the assembly of the *tiers* of the only corporation of workers regularly constituted and recognised', it was complained, 'show the state of mind of the bourgeoisie, which drew up *by itself* the *cahier* of the town and chose, *to the exclusion of every other influence*, the representatives of this great workers' city for the États Généraux.'[4]

At Pont l'Abbé the bourgeois rejected the grievances put forward by the artisans and peasants, and the latter withdrew to draw up their own *cahier*.[5] At Douarnenez, also in Brittany, the bourgeois accused the *sénéchal* of

---

[1] *Ibid.*, II, pp. 305, 451, 478.
[2] Bouloiseau, *Cahiers de Rouen*, I, p. lxxiii.
[3] *Ibid.*, II, p. 125.
[4] Laurent, *Reims et la région rémoise*, p. 126.
[5] Savina et Bernard, *Cahiers de Quimper et de Concarneau*, I, p. lvii.

admitting a tumultuous crowd of children, women, non-domiciled labourers, and seditious persons, some even drunk, to the electoral assembly, from which the bourgeois and merchants consequently withdrew.[1] At Rouen the poorer populace seems to have succeeded in expressing its views in a few *cahiers*.[2]

By and large, there can be no doubt that the propertied classes maintained their control of the electoral proceedings of 1789, and that any attempt by those they called—rather contemptuously—the 'people' to assert its rights or give expression to its grievances was met with severe and swift repression, and usually stifled at birth. The revolution was to be more ruthless than the *ancien régime* in its refusal to admit that the populace had any legitimate grievances, or that any governmental action was needed to remedy them.

[1] *Ibid.*
[2] *Cf.* Bouloiseau, *Cahiers de Rouen*, II, p. 333.

CHAPTER XIII

POOR AGAINST RICH

THE mixture of fear and contempt with which the men of property—at least above the level of the humblest small-holders—regarded the poorer and propertyless sections of society was accompanied by an organisation of defences against attack on their interests from below as vigorous as their own onslaught on the positions of power and prestige to which an effete noblesse had been clinging from above. If their hostility to the 'people' was now more conscious and more openly expressed than formerly, this was perhaps because they now had more to be afraid of. The inarticulate masses could not have been equally an object of fear before they became the masses, and this they did only with the rise in population, and especially urban population, in the course of the eighteenth century. They were also, if only to a very slight extent, ceasing to be totally inarticulate.

We must be careful, however, not to draw the wrong conclusions from these developments. The popular movement in the French Revolution has too often been envisaged in the light of ideas derived from the study of very different conditions in England, where social and political conditions had been diverging from those of France at least since the later centuries of the Middle Ages. In rural England the system of large landowner, substantial tenant farmer and agricultural labourer had established a social pattern which is only rarely to be found in France. This is why the application of presuppositions about commons and enclosures derived from English experience has led to such a radical misinterpretation of French agrarian history at the time of the revolution. Equally, in provincial towns like Bristol or Sheffield, as well as in London, there already existed, towards the end of the eighteenth century, a large wage-earning working-class, with an awareness of its economic interests and the rudiments of a political consciousness, capable of throwing up leaders on the level of national politics, such as the shoe-maker Thomas Hardy, or the tailor Francis Place; capable of creating, largely under the leadership of men like these, political organisations of working men with a coherent and rational political programme, such as the London Corresponding Society.

There is nothing surprising in the fact that, the economic development of English society being so far in advance of that of France, its political evolution should also have shown much greater maturity. The democratic movement in Great Britain, of which we can see the beginnings in the generation before the French Revolution, was to have during the subsequent century a practically unbroken history of the slow acquisition of political influence and improvement in economic welfare. The French Revolution, on the other hand, remained under middle-class, propertied leadership from beginning to end. Research on the *sans-culottes* has brought this out even more clearly than before. Talk about ruffians like the butcher Legendre or the brewer Santerre should not mislead us. Ruffians they may have been, but they were well-off, middle-class ruffians. When we come to the most advanced political and economic movement of the revolution, the Conspiracy of the Equals inspired by Babeuf, it proves to be one of the most thoroughly middle-class of the lot.

However, this does not end the question. 'Middle-class' is as large and indeterminate a description as bourgeois, and social tensions were not absent within the ranks of the more and the less propertied. Also, we have to ask if there is no evidence at all of movements from the wage-earning minority.

Denunciation of riches was a literary fashion in eighteenth-century France, derived partly from the influence of classical literature. Montesquieu, in his history of the Troglodytes, showed corruption coming in with the introduction of property and the growth of wealth. This was part of the literary campaign against luxury, inspired by moral and not economic ideas, but opposed on the ground of the economic advantages of luxury spending. Rousseau, in the *Discourse on Inequality*, provided the source and inspiration of much nineteenth-century equalitarianism; but there is no evidence that his Discourse was taken seriously in the eighteenth century, or regarded as anything more than an exercise in paradox like the First Discourse. Morelly, hardly read at the time and little more than a name now, Mably, Raynal, Diderot —these wrote literary exercises on the theme of equality, more or less sincere, but with no detectable social consequences.

On the eve of the revolution, we begin to find social

comment directed more specifically to actually existing conditions and inspired by either idealism or cynicism. The latter seems to have been the motive of the journalist Linguet, in whose writings there is an uncomfortably blunt recognition of facts. 'Do you not see', he writes, 'that the obedience, the total exploitation, to speak frankly, of a large part of the flock is responsible for the wealth of the shepherd? . . . Let them run senselessly at the mere sight of his [the sheep dog's] shadow. Everyone gains by it. You find it easier to herd them together to collect their fleece: they are better guaranteed from being eaten by wolves. True, it is only to be eaten by men, but anyhow that is their lot from the moment they came into the fold. Before talking of releasing them from it, begin by destroying the fold, that is to say, society!'[1] Again, 'The suppression of slavery involved no pretence of the suppression of wealth or its advantages. There was no thought of bringing men back to their original equality; the renunciation of their privileges by the rich was only a pretence. Things tend to remain as they always were, and slavery is perpetuated on earth, though under a less harsh name. . . . Town and country are peopled with a race of men known as *journaliers*, *manœuvriers*, etc. They never share in the abundance that their labour creates. . . . This race of men is undoubtedly the most numerous section of every nation. What has it gained by the suppression of slavery? The slave was fed, even when he did not work, as horses have hay on holidays. . . . But what

[1] H. Linguet, *Théorie des loix civiles ou principes fondamentaux de la société* (1767), cited in J. Cruppi, *Un avocat journaliste au XVIIIe siècle: Linguet* (1895), p. 164.

is the fate of the *manœuvre libre*, who is often badly paid when he works, when he does not work?'[1]

We must not let Linguet mislead us with all this. He is no reformer, but rather a reactionary, who makes a parade of his recognition of hard facts for the purpose of showing how useless it is to hope to improve them. 'What is the good', he asks, 'of these sentimental affectations, these plans of reform in finance and taxation? What is the use of parliamentarism, of institutions from the political system of England? What is the use of the intermediary bodies praised by Montesquieu, of these greedy judicial corporations which, under the pretext of restricting royal power, only protect their own privileges and multiply the instruments of tyranny? What is the good of all this, since the poor must always be oppressed by the rich, and he who works must always be at the service of him who possesses? One tyrant is better than a thousand tyrants!'[2]

Linguet, who must be accounted a journalist rather than a serious social or political thinker, may be, for this reason, all the more significant. His one tyrant, who is preferable to a thousand, can hardly be a reference to poor Louis XVI; it is much more like an anticipation of Napoleon. He reflects, consciously or not, the bitterness of relations between the richer and the poorer sections of society, the resentments of the poor and the harsh reaction of the rich, that were to be let loose by the social and political dissolution that accompanied the revolution. Examples only can be given of the widespread denuncia-

[1] *Ibid.*, p. 166.
[2] *Ibid.*, pp. 168–9.

tion of the rich that one finds in the *cahiers*, pamphlets, journals and popular literature of 1789 and the following years.

An analysis of this literature of denunciation might begin with general attacks on the rich. For example: 'There are many men who by their wealth alone have acquired privileges of which the rest of the *tiers état* is the victim';[1] 'as soon as a rich man finds himself at his ease and has his comforts, he always looks round to see how he can oppress the poor *menu peuple*';[2] 'the rich do no charitable works, or very little, and leave the poor to groan while they live in luxury.'[3] The wealth of the clergy was a particular object of attack, especially where, as in Reims, they were the great landowners.[4] 'What an abundant recourse', says one anti-clerical *cahier*, 'would the government not find in these rich abbeys, these priories, these chapters, these communities of either sex.'[5] The huge revenues of the convents should be used to liquidate the debts of the state, and their inmates put to useful work in the parishes, which are short of priests.[6] The lesser clergy themselves were not immune from dangerous thoughts. The '*églisiers, soutaniers* and priests of the parishes of Paris', to adopt their own description (but the source of this document may be only a small discontented minority), complain that the ministry is reserved for '*les gens comme il faut*', that is to say, the rich. 'It is in

[1] Mège, *Cahiers d'Auvergne*, p. 194.
[2] Boissonade, *Cahiers d'Angoulême*, pp. 157–8.
[3] C. Étienne, *Cahiers de doléances des bailliages des généralités de Metz et de Nancy* (1912), ii, pp. 239–40.
[4] Laurent, *Reims et la région rémoise*, p. 109.
[5] Desplaces de Charmasse, *Cahiers d'Autun*, p. 163.
[6] Savina et Bernard, *Cahiers de Quimper et de Concarneau*, i, p. 272.

weight of gold that they measure the importance of their parishioners; the poor are not worthy of their attention.'[1]

More significant than vague denunciations of wealth is the concentration of the attack on speculative gains. When there still survived relics of the idea that everything had a just price, the making of profits out of short-term variations in price seemed peculiarly shocking. Hence the widespread and continuous criticism of those guilty of 'that odious refinement of usury and greed known as *agiotage*.'[2] Usurers and speculators should be exposed to public indignation.[3] 'Let those men sufficiently degraded to prostitute themselves to the game of speculation be declared enemies of the nation and unworthy of the name of merchants',[4] declares the *tiers* of Lyon. 'The merchant', says a *cahier* of the *sénéchaussée* of Cahors, 'is no longer, today, hard-working, economical, watching over his business; he is a sort of modern tax-farmer, who lives at the height of luxury.'[5]

France, it must be remembered, was still a Roman Catholic country, where usury was officially under the ban of the church. Loans at interest were legally proscribed until 12 October 1789,[6] though this did not mean that they were not made. The *cahiers* of the clergy called for their prohibition.[7] The noblesse, on the other hand, wanted interest to be legalised but restricted to a modest

---

[1] Chassin, *Cahiers de Paris*, II, p. 96.
[2] *Ibid.*, II, p. 65.
[3] *Ibid.*, II, p. 457.
[4] F. Grille, *Introduction aux Mémoires*, II, p. 203.
[5] Fourastié, *Cahiers de Cahors*, pp. 279–80.
[6] *Cf.* Forster, *Nobility of Toulouse*, p. 106.
[7] Grille, *Introduction aux Mémoires*, II, p. 194 *seqq.*

rate—5% was usually suggested.[1] The *tiers état* seems less concerned about usury—perhaps they had already come to take it for granted.

The attack on speculation had a more specific cause than the generalised hostility to wealth. Land values were rising in the eighteenth century and bringing monied men, small and large, into the competition for land. Their intervention was all the more resented because of the prevailing land hunger caused by the increase in population. Financially, the decade before the revolution was one of speculative mania, nourished by government borrowing at high rates of interest to cope with the expenses of the American War. The bankers of Europe— Swiss, Austrian, German, Dutch and Walloon, English— descended on Paris.[2] The Farmers General, because of their responsibility for the indirect taxes, which they were collecting with an increased efficiency which did not enhance their popularity, were the most hated of all the financiers. 'They are the leeches of the state, a vermin which devours it, a pest which infests it.'[3] Speculation was held responsible for the shortage of grain and its high price.[4] The depression in manufactures was attributed to the same cause.[5]

One of the chief grievances, as has been said above, was that the monied men—*gens à portefeuille*—escaped taxation. The nobles particularly emphasise this, perhaps

[1] *Ibid.*

[2] *Cf.* J. Bouchary, *Les Manieurs d'argent à la fin du XVIIIe siècle*, 3 vol. (1939, 1940, 1943).

[3] Bouloiseau, *Cahiers de Rouen*, II, p. 308.

[4] *Ibid.*, II, p. 340; Chassin, *Cahiers de Paris*, II, p. 472; IV, p. 14.

[5] Jouanne, *Cahiers d'Alençon*, pp. 60-1.

hoping to get their own back on them.[1] There were also demands that the burden of taxation should not fall only on owners of land.[2] When the Constituent Assembly drew up its new scheme of taxation, the marquis de Ferrières feared that the result would be to crush the landed proprietors, 'for the capitalists aim to pay nothing and they will achieve their object'.[3]

His language reminds us that this was the period in which 'capitalist' came into use as a term of contempt. It meant the new rich, the shady financiers (*brasseurs en banque*), and all those who made money by financial operations.[4] Those who were primarily landowners, industrialists, or overseas merchants, did not come into the same category. The survival of older economic attitudes into the revolution is exhibited in the assertion of Rivarol: 'The favour with which government looks on its subjects should always be in inverse ratio to the mobility of their wealth. Thus the one who should be most favoured is the *laboureur*. . . . I put in the lowest rank the monied man, who, like a magician, can with a stroke of the pen transport his wealth to the ends of the world, and who, never operating except with tokens, equally gives nature and society the slip. The government owes nothing to such a man.'[5]

So far, all our examples of protests against the abuse of wealth have come from within the ranks of property.

[1] Grille, *Introduction aux Mémoires*, II, pp. 311–12.

[2] Bouloiseau, *Cahiers de Rouen*, II, p. 190; Bligny-Bondurand, *Cahiers de Nîmes*, I, pp. 205, 274.

[3] Marquis de Ferrières, *Correspondance inédite*, p. 306.

[4] Labasse, *Le commerce des soies à Lyon*, p. 31.

[5] Rivarol, *Mémoires*, p. 181; cited in Bigo, *Les Bases historiques de la finance moderne*, p. 193.

The *cahiers* of the rural parishes occasionally reveal the wishes of an unpropertied proletariat. In the *bailliage* of Rouen, says M. Bouloiseau, the class struggle can be seen everywhere in the rural *cahiers*:[1] the richer farmer with surplus products to sell, the tithe-owner, the possessor of seigniorial rights, gained from the rise in prices on the eve of the revolution, while the great majority of the rural population suffered.[2] Jaurès noted that the division between the bourgeoisie and the people was more marked in 1789 in the country than in the town.[3] I would agree if the terms poorer and richer are substituted for people and bourgeoisie, and indeed the peasant movements of 1789 are described by a contemporary as 'a war declared by the poor against the rich'.[4] A letter to Necker, of 22 April 1789, said that the hostility of the peasants was directed against all who seemed to be over it. 'The *haut tiers*, nearest to it, has been the most attacked.'[5] But within the ranks of the peasants there was another, and perhaps even greater gulf, between those who did, and those who did not, possess any land. The village proletariat shared the farmers' hatred of the towns and the seigniorial *fermiers*, but added its own resentments against the land-owning *laboureurs*.[6] The demand for *partage* revealed momentarily the aspirations aroused, only to be frustrated, in the landless rural workers.

Another cause of division in rural society is revealed by

[1] Bouloiseau, *Cahiers de Rouen*, I, p. clxi.
[2] Lefebvre, *Études*, p. 165.
[3] J. Jaurès, *La Constituante (1789–1791)*, pp. 220, 272, 276.
[4] J. Egret, 'La prérévolution en Provence 1787–89', *Annales historiques de la Révolution française*, no. 135 (1954), p. 124.
[5] *Ibid.*
[6] Saint-Jacob, *Paysans de la Bourgogne*, p. 572.

the widespread protests against the existence of large farms. These predominated round Versailles, in the plain of Picardy, perhaps in Beauce and Brie, and elsewhere.[1] Of all the demands of the peasants up to the year II, says Lefebvre, the most obstinate was that for the division of the larger farms.[2] The Committee of Agriculture was inundated with petitions on this subject.[3] 'Read the title deeds of large properties', advises one *cahier*, 'you will see that most are composed of small properties which have been annexed in all kinds of ways. A peasant in hard times is dazzled with the offer of ready cash; difficulties are brought upon him by a cruel generosity in lending to him until he cannot repay what he has borrowed. Then his land is seized and sold at a low price to the advantage of the creditor.'[4] Another *cahier* demands a law compelling land to be divided into small farms 'as in former times', so that it will provide more work.[5] *Cahiers* in the *bailliage* of Rouen call for *laboureurs* to be prohibited from having more than one farm. 'Farmers', says a *cahier*, 'coqs de paroisse*, lease and occupy a series of small farms, sublet the buildings and only work the arable land, which prevents many of the king's subjects from setting up in their own establishments.' So the sons of independent farmers are reduced to the level of simple day-labourers—*manœuvriers*.[6] The *cahier* of Serres-en-Brie speaks of 'the

---

[1] Lefebvre, *Études*, p. 211.

[2] *Ibid.*

[3] *Cf.* Gerbaux et Schmidt, *Comités d'agriculture et de commerce.*

[4] Chassin, *Les élections et les cahiers de Paris*, IV, p. 176.

[5] *Ibid.*

[6] Gerbaux et Schmidt, *Comités d'agriculture et de commerce*, I, p. 91; Chassin, *Les élections et les cahiers de Paris*, IV, pp. 175–6, 271; Bouloiseau, *Cahiers de Rouen*, II, pp. 250, 300, 350, 364, 370, 373, 385; Loriquet, *Cahiers du Pas-de-Calais*, II, p. 353.

harsh servitude to which the rural workers are reduced by rich farmers who occupy up to three farms or more'.[1] Another claims that the most stuck-up (*huppés*) farmers, who now drive in their cabriolets, thirty or forty years ago rode on nags worth only three or four louis.[2]

To preserve a sense of proportion we must remember, of course, that even the large farms were not very large. All these complaints represent the discontent of agricultural workers, small-holders, or subsistence farmers against those who were a little above them in the social scale. To the middle-class townsman they were all peasants. Also, as has been indicated above, it was only in certain parts of France, where geographical conditions and the proximity of a large market were predisposing factors, that farms on any large scale may have developed. If the large farmer had been a less rare phenomenon, the French countryside might have been less profoundly conservative, and French agriculture less backward and unproductive.

In the towns the poorer elements of the population were less vocal and their sentiments are more difficult to discover than in the rural parishes. In the *bailliage* of Rouen, thirty *cahiers* out of 154 are favourable to the 'Fourth Estate'. These pass in silence over the question of political and administrative reforms, and concentrate on complaints of poverty.[3] Paris produces a few documents with such labels as '*Doléances du pauvre peuple*', written in the name of '*manœuvriers, journaliers, artisans et autres,*

---

[1] Chassin, *Les élections et les cahiers de Paris*, IV, p. 175.
[2] *Ibid.*
[3] Bouloiseau, *Cahiers de Rouen*, I, p. cli.

deprived of all property; or *cahier* of the Fourth Order'—
'*cette classe immense de journaliers, de salariés, de non gagés*';
or '*Pétition de 150,000 ouvriers et artisans de Paris*'.[1] How
far, if at all, any of these are genuine cannot be said. Most
probably they were literary exercises.

As regards genuine movements of wage-earners, it has
been said that the Réveillon riots of April 1789 are the
only insurrectionary movement of wage-earners in the
revolution.[2] This should not be taken to mean that there
were no other independent wage-earners' movements.
The concentration of interest on political action has, however, directed the attention of historians away from such
movements as there were, and political extremism had
curiously little social content or connection with any
demand for social reform. Indeed, the *sans-culottist* movement diverted the agitation of the populace away from
wage demands, perhaps not unintentionally. The Committee of Public Safety imposed a *maximum* on wages,
though how far it was observed is unknown. Lefebvre
cites the case of a staunch Jacobin mayor in whose *commune* the *maximum* was at its lowest: true he was also a
well-to-do farmer.[3]

In local studies incidental signs of wage movements
appear here and there. There was an agitation of workers
in the naval arsenals early in the revolution.[4] Expressions
of discontent such as this may have succeeded in driving
up nominal wages during the revolution, but real wages

---

[1] Picard, *Les cahiers de 1789*, p. 45.
[2] Rudé, *The Crowd in the French Revolution*, p. 39.
[3] Lefebvre, *Paysans du Nord*, p. 652.
[4] N. Hampson, *La marine de l'an II* (1959), p. 48.

probably fell.[1] Again, the unrest of 1789 stirred up some of the journeymen of Paris, the *garçons perruquiers*, *garçons tailleurs*, *garçons boulangers*, to attempt to break away from their masters and set up for themselves. They demonstrated before the town hall, but the significant comment is, 'They were not listened to.'[2] In the spring of 1791 strikes, especially by *compagnon* carpenters, who were attempting to obtain a wage scale from the Paris municipality to enforce on the employers, alarmed the bourgeoisie and led to the passing of the law Le Chapelier on 14 June 1791.[3]

In the years just before the revolution a more persistent agitation had developed in the textile areas against the introduction of spinning machinery from England. It produced an occasional Luddite outbreak such as the riot at Falaise in 1788, which was provoked by the setting up of a spinning mill.[4] The *cahiers* of the Rouen area exhibit a particularly widespread demand for the destruction of machines, though such a demand also appears elsewhere.[5] The complaint was always, of course, that they put labour out of work, especially—and this is a sign of its importance—that of women and children. The most significant feature of the agitation for the suppression of the new machines is that it appears both in the general

[1] Lefebvre, review of P. Léon, *La naissance de la grande industrie en Dauphiné*, *Annales historiques de la Révolution française*, no. 140 (1955), pp. 289–90.

[2] L. Scheler, *Lavoisier et la Révolution française*, II. *Le journal de Fougeroux de Bondaroy* (1960), pp. 159–60.

[3] Soboul, *Précis*, p. 157.

[4] Jouanne, *Cahiers d'Alençon*, p. lxiii.

[5] Bouloiseau, *Cahiers de Rouen*, I, pp. 62, 66 and *passim*; II, pp. 19, 21, 22, 34 and *passim*; Picard, *Les cahiers de 1789*, pp. 110–11; Chassin, *Les élections et les cahiers de Paris*, II, p. 484.

cahiers of the parishes and in those of the corporations of
Rouen. The architects, public letter-writers, apothe-
caries, bakers, beer and cider sellers, cooks and pastry
makers, hatters, locksmiths, farriers, and so on are as
opposed to the introduction of machines as those who
were liable to be thrown out of employment by them.[1]
What is reflected in all these is not humanitarian sentiment, but the economic and social conservatism of a
society that, however prepared it may have been for
political revolution, was determined to cling to the
economic methods to which it was accustomed. The
stone and marble cutters of Paris demand the suppression
of a machine because it enables two men to do the work of
ninety.[2] Machines suit the English, say the hatters of
Rouen, because of the commerce resulting from their
great colonial possessions; they are not needed in France.
If, as a result of the suppression of machines, French manufactures are a little dearer than foreign ones, this must be
accepted.[3] The important thing that all this reveals is not
the actual destruction of machines—this seems to have
been rather rare—but the evidence of a general conservative attitude of mind, in the propertied as well as the poor
who might lose employment, a widespread spirit of hostility to economic change.

Perhaps the most acute, and certainly the most vocal, of
the internal divisions in urban society at the time of the
revolution was that between the master craftsmen or the
artisans, and the merchant class which was obtaining a

[1] Bouloiseau, *loc. cit.*
[2] Chassin, *Les élections et les cahiers de Paris*, II, p. 484.
[3] Bouloiseau, *Cahiers de Rouen*, I, p. 114.

stranglehold over their trades, in some cases by using the competition of cheaper rural labour against them.[1] In Lyon, where, before the revolution, the master silk-weavers had fallen into dependence on the merchants, who controlled both the supplies of raw material and the outlets for the finished article, a violent hatred had developed[2] which manifested itself in bitter struggles during the eighteenth century, as it was to do again in the nineteenth. The revolutionary period, when both merchants and masters suffered from the collapse of trade and turned equally against the revolutionary government, was one of lull in this social war.

One small example, out of many, of this type of social conflict may be taken from the little Breton fishing port of Concarneau. Here the fishermen complained that 'rich merchants' were obtaining control and exploiting them. The method was to buy up on the spot, or even by sending agents to Norway, the *rogue*—salted cod's roe used as bait—which was then retailed to the fishermen at exorbitant prices—three times, they said, what they had paid twenty years earlier.[3] The middlemen had also obtained control of the sales of the sardine fisheries;[4] and more recently had even begun to purchase boats. This intrusion into the fish trade was proving so profitable, it was said, that *avocats*, *procureurs*, tax-collectors, as well as merchants, were investing in fishing boats at Concarneau, as they already did at Douarnenez.[5] A letter from the

[1] Sée, *L'Évolution commerciale et industrielle*, pp. 310, 311, 315.
[2] *Ibid.*
[3] Savina et Bernard, *Cahiers de Quimper et de Concarneau*, pp. 231, 294, 300.
[4] *Ibid.*, p. 304.
[5] *Ibid.*, p. 79.

sénéchal of Concarneau supported the complaints of the *cahiers*.[1]

These are quarrels among those who own property, however small it may have been in some cases. We may well suspect, below the ranks of the master-weavers of Lyon, or the small fishing-boat owners of Concarneau, the existence, silent and submerged, of a proletariat who owned nothing. Against them, the ranks of property, however violent their internecine struggles, would always be closed if they attempted to assert their interests. During the revolutionary and Napoleonic period there is little sign that they ever did. In the town, as in the country, if we can pass any general verdict on social developments at this time, it would be that they consolidated the claims of property against the propertyless and of the richer, on all levels, against the poorer.

[1] *Ibid.*, pp. 307–9.

CHAPTER XIV

CONCLUSION

THROUGHOUT this book I have been discussing the problems involved in writing the social history of the revolution. In doing so I have not intended to suggest that it was other than primarily a political revolution, a struggle for the possession of power and over the conditions in which power was to be exercised. Essentially the revolution was the overthrow of the old political system of the monarchy and the creation of a new one in the shape of the Napoleonic state. However, behind the political régime there is always the social structure, which is in a sense more fundamental and is certainly much more difficult to change. Once we begin to investigate this social background to the revolution, it is borne in on us how little notice ordinary political history has taken of it, and indeed how little we really know of the actual pattern of eighteenth-century French society and the impact on it of the revolution. The supposed social categories of our histories—bourgeois, aristocrats, sans-culottes—are all in fact political ones. Three-quarters of a century of revolutionary historical research, including much comment on the movement of social groupings, has been conducted under the influence of ideas derived from politics, transferring its categories to the context of social history. This research has itself in the end exploded

the ideas which inspired it, and demonstrated the in-
adequacy of the social terminology employed and the
politico-sociological theories it reflects. We know now
that there was a much more complicated social pattern in
eighteenth-century France than has commonly been
recognised and that it demands a more sophisticated historical analysis.

Every attempt at historical interpretation, new or old,
must stand or fall by its consistency with the evidence. I
have tried to show that there is much even in the present
state of knowledge of the revolution which is irreconcil-
able with the accepted interpretation, and to offer some
suggestions towards a possible alternative. This book was
written before I was able to read Lefebvre's valuable
posthumously published study of the social structure of
Orléans on the eve of the revolution.[1] Although I would
certainly have drawn on Lefebvre's material in the course
of this study if his book had appeared in time, there is a
certain advantage in being able to use it only in the con-
cluding chapter. His analysis of the society of Orléans
can serve as a kind of test case by which to judge the
validity of some of the main ideas that have been put
forward in the preceding chapters. This will be all the
more valuable in that Lefebvre himself was sincerely and
unquestionably attached to the orthodox theory of the
revolution and saw no contradiction between his theory
and the historical facts he had uncovered.

The first point that is bound to strike the reader is that
in the Orléanais the revolution *qua* attack on feudalism

---

[1] G. Lefebvre, *Études Orléanaises*, i. *Contribution à l'étude des structures sociales
à la fin du XVIIIe siècle* (1962).

seems remarkably muted. The seigniorial system plays a minor role among the grievances of the peasantry.[1] It seems reasonable to conclude that this was not one of the areas in which it constituted a heavy burden. As has been suggested in earlier chapters, the most general attacks were on *franc-fief* and on the *banalités*.[2] The former Lefebvre links with the passage of large areas of noble land into the possession of *roturiers*;[3] while he associates the latter with the peasant suspicion of the extortions of the millers.[4] Both, therefore, belong with the abuses of the newer commercial rather than the older feudal structure.

The same resentment against the intrusion of commercial motives into the countryside is to be detected in the hatred of the large farmers, who, it was said, monopolised land on which a much larger number of small men might have had their little holdings. The result, declared one *cahier*, repeating many complaints that have been cited above, was that the sons of *laboureurs*, unable to set themselves up on independent holdings, had to remain on the family farm, while their daughters went into service; after which both were reduced to marrying below them (*après que tous ont fini par se mésallier*) and sinking into the ranks of the poor.[5] The class structure of rural France also emerges here, as well as the resentment of a peasantry accustomed in the main to subsistence farming against the intrusion of a capitalist way of life.

---

[1] *Cf. ibid.*, pp. 64–74.
[2] *Ibid.*, pp. 66–7.
[3] *Ibid.*, p. 66.
[4] *Ibid.*, pp. 244, 255.
[5] *Ibid.*, p. 24 n. 25; *cf.* pp. 23–4, 34.

The *grands fermiers* were also denounced in the Orléan-ais as 'farmers' in another sense, who farmed the tithe and the seigniorial dues.[1] As elsewhere, the penetration of urban wealth into the country is revealed by bourgeois ownership of land, especially in the neighbourhood of towns.[2] The peasant complaints of 'financiers' from the towns[3] are added to their widespread suspicion of all who engaged in commerce, and in the liberal professions, and in fact of townspeople as a whole.[4]

The picture that Lefebvre gives us of the social struc-ture and stresses in the Orléanais countryside thus con-forms in its main lines with that reached earlier in this book. Here also we meet once again the attempt to reconcile it with the orthodox theory of a 'bourgeois revolt against feudalism' by the invention of a class of *'bourgeoisie paysanne'* or *'bourgeoisie rurale'*, which is to be found, Lefebvre says at one point, in the *bourgs*, where it is composed of bourgeois proper or *rentiers*, notaries, the post-master, doctors, surgeons, surveyors, bailiffs;[5] but on another page it becomes an amalgam of peasant pro-prietors and merchants;[6] and yet again reverts to being rentiers, or merchants, a surgeon, and officers of the local court, such as the clerk, notary, bailiff.[7] The picture is as confused as ever, and the situation is not improved when Lefebvre, turning his gaze from the small towns to the

---

[1] *Ibid.*, p. 25.
[2] *Ibid.*, pp. 21, 33.
[3] *Ibid.*, p. 64, n. 161.
[4] *Ibid.*, p. 73.
[5] *Ibid.*, p. 26.
[6] *Ibid.*, p. 45.
[7] *Ibid.*, p. 53.

country, has honestly to admit that the rural bourgeoisie is difficult to find there at all.[1]

The conclusion to which we found ourselves forced, though Lefebvre does not draw it, was that the structure of *ancien régime* society was a good deal more complex than was allowed for in the simple pattern of bourgeois and feudalism. He does, in another connection, recognise the problem of social terminology. In discussing a decree of the King's Council affecting the corporative organisation of the hosiery manufacture in Orléans he points out that the terms used in the *arrêt* do not correspond either with current usage at the time or with social and economic realities. The *négociants*, who had obtained control of the industry, were also impartially called *fabricants* or *marchands*, while the artisans were in effect simple employees for wages.[2] This, indeed, carries us a little farther than anything that has been instanced above, for, as Lefebvre says, it shows the corporative system being used 'as a means of reinforcing legally the control of the capitalist entrepreneur'.[3] The general verdict on French society at the end of the *ancien régime* with which he concludes is that class distinctions were as sharp, and in some respects sharper, than today.[4] Towards the populace the bourgeois exhibited the same *hauteur* and often the same contempt as they complained of experiencing themselves from the noblesse.[5] In their *cahiers* they called for stricter legal controls over their workers.[6] On

[1] *Ibid.*, pp. 35, 45.
[2] *Ibid.*, p. 220.
[3] *Ibid.*, p. 221.
[4] *Ibid.*, p. 226.
[5] *Ibid.*, p. 227.
[6] *Ibid.*, p. 225.

the other hand, higher up in the scale social distinctions were evidently becoming blurred. A memoir of the *juge-conseils* of Orléans revealed that the *négociants* included '*gentilhommes*' in their ranks, and that many more of them enjoyed the privileges of noblesse by virtue of royal grant or the purchase of the office of *secrétaire du roi*.[1]

In conclusion it must be said that nothing in Lefebvre's last work is inconsistent with the revisions in the interpretation of the revolution that I have suggested. On the contrary his new material seems to me to confirm and reinforce the argument of this book. It shows that the grievances of the lower and therefore more dissatisfied elements in town and country were not so much against the survival of an old feudal order of society as against the coming of a newer capitalist one. Lefebvre himself sees the same factors at work in town and country. The question of food supplies, he suggests, was not what primarily set them at enmity with one another. Taken by itself this assertion may be regarded as doubtful, though even in claiming that the conflict between town and country was only subsidiary, Lefebvre tacitly admits its existence. We may think that it was more fundamental than he allows, but at the same time agree that along with it can be detected a different, and what might even be regarded as a sort of class, struggle. 'Artisans and shop-keepers had the same point of view as proletarians,' writes Lefebvre, 'the small peasant proprietors as the day-labourers; both professors of law and clergy condemned speculation.'[2] Socially, he concludes, there was a struggle

[1] *Ibid.*, p. 201.
[2] *Ibid.*, p. 261.

against rising capitalism, though he does not seem to realise the implications of his argument for the theory of the 'bourgeois revolution'. The effect must be, I think, to confirm the view which I have put forward that the revolution was to an important extent one *against* and not *for* the rising forces of capitalism. In addition it can be interpreted, as I have also said above, in terms of a general tension and social antagonism between the poor and the rich. Once again, therefore, Lefebvre can be called to our assistance, even though it is in support of a thesis that he would have repudiated.

One object of this study has been to suggest, by providing a positive example, the possibility of an empirical approach to the writing of social history, which will enable it to escape from the rigid patterns of system-makers who have deduced their history from their theories. The relation of social theory to social history should be, it seems to me, similar to the relation of political and economic theories respectively to political and economic history. Each of these theoretical disciplines was evolved after consideration of an extensive range of historical experience. Their terminology is therefore relevant to the task of the historian. A particular weakness of most social theory on the contrary, especially from the point of view of its applicability to history, has been its neglect of historical evidence and its almost exclusive dependence on a small range of contemporary material. This not only means that it has developed a language which is inappropriate to past conditions, it also means that it usually deals either with a static situation or else with one involving only very short-term changes.

History, on the other hand, requires perspective, which cannot be achieved by concentrating on the developments of a few months or even a few years.

What has been written on the social history of the revolutionary period has suffered from both these defects. It adopted as its model a sociological theory derived from the circumstances of a later age, and it used for the purpose of historical analysis the events of a mere year or two. This interpretation was then projected backwards and forwards, and the histories of the previous and the following centuries were twisted out of shape by the influence of the same arbitrary pattern. To fit in with the theory, eighteenth-century France had to be envisaged as still basically a feudal society, but one which was to become after the revolution predominantly capitalist and industrial, regardless of the facts. Thus Lefebvre could write of 'the terrible conditions into which large-scale industry was going to precipitate the working-class in the course of the following decades'[1]—ignoring the terrible conditions, and numbers, of the poor in 1789, which he himself had described, and assuming the appearance in France of a large-scale industry in the early years of the nineteenth century, which his theory required but the facts, alas, repudiated.

If, on the other hand, we look with an open mind on the society that emerged from the revolution, we will be most struck by the permanent elements in the French social pattern. We will see a society with many new elements it is true, but bearing on it like a palimpsest the inadequately effaced writing of the *ancien régime*. The whole

[1] Lefebvre, *Études*, p. 261.

development of French society appears in a different light if we recognise that the revolution was a triumph for the conservative, propertied, land-owning classes, large and small. This was one of the factors—of course not the only one—contributing to the economic backwardness of France in the following century. It helps us to see that in the course of the revolution the social hierarchy, modified and based more openly on wealth, particularly landed wealth, and political influence, and less on birth and aristocratic connections, was strengthened and re-asserted. Again, it is true that the revolution brought about important humanitarian reforms, and eliminated innumerable traditional barriers to the more unified and politically more efficient modern state: but it also frustrated the movement for a better treatment of the poorest sections of society, both rural and urban, which was manifesting itself in the last years of the *ancien régime*. The agricultural proletariat, says Lefebvre, suffered from the revolution.[1] The charitable activities of the church in the eighteenth century (and these should not be under-estimated) were largely brought to an end; the *biens de charité* were incorporated in the *biens nationaux* in the year II and until 29 fructidor year III went to swell the property of the purchasers of church lands.[2] For the poor, possibly a harsher governmental climate was in-augurated. Whoever won the revolution, they lost.

I am really saying nothing new here, and nothing that the historians in the great revolutionary tradition have not said themselves. But having been said, it has usually

[1] *Ibid.*, p. 260.
[2] Lefebvre, *Paysans du Nord*, pp. 738–40.

been put on one side and forgotten, because the possibility that a revolution of the people—an ambiguous term—might have to be regarded as having had unhappy results for the people themselves could not be contemplated. The revolution was by definition a good thing. If any bad things seemed to be involved in it, then they were not part of it, or did not really exist. The revolution became a Sorelian myth, as Georges Lefebvre in the end proclaimed.[1] As the heroic age of French republicanism its record must not be sullied. As the mother of revolutions to come, to use M. Guérin's phrase, it was to be treated with filial solicitude. It represented an earlier stage on the road that civilisation had to follow. To see it as in any way a diversion, or even a reversal of the one-way traffic dictated by the laws of a great philosophy of history, was too shocking to consider.

Even when evidence that might have led to a different interpretation of the revolution was adduced, it was forced into the pre-conceived pattern. Lefebvre argues that the economic interpretation of history is given an unduly narrow form when the revolution is regarded as the result simply of the rise of the bourgeoisie. It also came, he says, from the resistance of the privileged to the birth of a new economic order, and the opposition of the least-favoured classes to the coming capitalist society. The grudge of the latter against the aristocracy, he agrees, was not only because the feudal order had always oppressed them, but also because the capitalist spirit was penetrating into the aristocracy itself and rendering it more odious. Most of this is true, though it is not the whole

[1] Lefebvre, 'Le Mythe de la révolution française', pp. 344–5.

truth; but his conclusion is that though in this way the germination of a new social order provoked hostile reactions, at the same time these favoured its triumph. That this view is a little illogical might not matter, but it also assumes that the new social order hypothesised did in fact triumph.

I have tried to show that the social developments of the revolution are capable of a very different and even an entirely contrary interpretation, that it was not wholly a revolution for, but largely one against, the penetration of an embryo capitalism into French society. Considered as such, it largely achieved its ends. The peasant proprietors in the country, and the lawyers, *rentiers* and men of property in the towns, successfully resisted the new economic trends. The latter, in particular, took control of the revolution and consolidated their régime by the dictatorship of Napoleon. 'United to what remained of the old noblesse', says Lefebvre, 'it [the bourgeoisie] constituted henceforth a landed aristocracy powerful enough to hold down, under its economic dictatorship, that rural democracy which it had in part created.'[1]

In so far as capitalist economic developments were at issue, it was a revolution not for, but against, capitalism. This would, I believe, have been recognised long ago if it had not been for the influence of an unhistorical sociological theory. The misunderstanding was facilitated by the ambiguities implicit in the idea of the bourgeoisie. The bourgeois of the theory are a class of capitalists, industrial entrepreneurs and financiers of big business; those of the French Revolution were landowners, *rentiers*

[1] Lefebvre, *Études*, p. 261.

and officials, including in their fish-pond a few big fish, many of moderate size, and a host of minnows, who all knew that they swam in the same element, and that without the pervasive influence of the social hierarchy and the maintenance of individual and family property rights against any interference by the state, their way of life, confined, unchanging, conservative, repetitive, would come to an end. The revolution was theirs, and for them at least it was a wholly successful revolution.

INDEX

Index

Index